The COMING COLLISION

Global Law vs. U.S. Liberties

JAMES L. HIRSEN, PH.D.

BRIDGER HOUSE PUBLISHERS, INC.

Published By:
Bridger House Publishers, Inc.
PO Box 599, Hayden ID, USA 83835
1-800-729-4131   www.nohoax.com

Library of Congress Card Catalog Number 98-74022

ISBN: 978-1-893157-02-6

Published in the United States

Contents

Introduction

The world is a rapidly changing place. Incidents that most people would find unbelievable are occurring beyond the public view and outside the concern of the mainstream press. Events that have already transpired, and those that are presently being planned, have deep significance for our personal lives and profound implications for our nation.

Men and women in all walks of life are concerned about and frustrated over the erosion of individual freedom, infringement of private property rights, and suppression of religious expression that is apparent in our society today. What many may not realize, though, is that destructive influences that have detrimentally affected communities and institutions within our nation are now permeating our country from an outside origin. Disturbing and undesirable ideas are being thrust upon us in a deceptive and stealthy manner from an unexpected source known as "international law."

In this book, the intricacies of international law are explored in depth, exposing the strong connection between an elite, worldwide group of bureaucrats and current applications of international law. Like-minded power brokers operating at the highest levels of government have a broad and ambitious agenda, and they are working diligently to implement their plans. What does this mean for average, everyday American citizens? The political, legal, social, and moral implications of these global maneuverings are vigorously examined in the pages that follow, and the direct impact upon our daily lives is revealed.

A subject that is largely unfamiliar to the general public involves treaty power. It falls under the domain of the federal government and contains information that most people believe has little effect on them. However, a closer look reveals a very different picture. Congress is in the business of passing federal statutes.

When federal law is ineffective at the state level, treaties can be utilized to accomplish a desired result by invoking international legal principles. Congressional history has supplied us with fascinating illustrations that demonstrate how the convoluted interpretation and misapplication of international law can easily occur. The fallout of such circumvention is extremely relevant to anyone concerned with protecting the integrity of our system of government.

Interestingly enough, our founding fathers had serious concerns about and struggles with this very subject. Undoubtedly in anticipation of circumstances such as those we presently face, they sought to limit governmental power despite the demands of foreign policy. Unfortunately, too many judges in America today are unaware of the intentions of the founding fathers regarding the legal effects of treaties upon domestic affairs. This apparent lack of knowledge and understanding on the part of our judiciary regarding contemplated uses of international law leaves our country in a vulnerable and precarious situation.

The reality that the imposition of international treaties threatens fundamental liberties came to the forefront in the 1950s. The result was a proposal to amend the Constitution and limit the burgeoning body of treaty law that affected domestic, economic, and social behavior. A battle ensued involving forces that actually gave birth to those that will be on the front lines of the coming collision.

Americans need to be aware of what global bureaucrats already know. There is a growing body of agreements with the benign-sounding label of *soft law* operating at the international level. Soft law includes such things as declarations, agreements, resolutions, summits, and the like. These are, in actuality, unenforceable agreements between nations. A clear pattern exists, however, to show that such measures have a way of slowly evolving into enforceable, international law. Needless to say, the consequences to national sovereignty can be devastating.

Items that have additionally contributed to the reduction of American sovereignty are interlaced within the GATT and NAFTA trade agreements. The requirement of a two-thirds vote by the Senate was ignored when Congress ratified these so-called executive agreements. Executive agreements are treaties in disguise, but they lack the usual constitutional safeguards. It is not impossible that staggering proposals, such as an international criminal court or global tax, might slip in under the cover of soft law, executive agreement, or treaty.

Former Communists, liberal politicians, New Age leaders, occult practitioners, feminists, globalists, and other diverse individuals are racing to embrace the cause of environmentalism. Alarm bells should go off when such an eclectic group coalesces, especially since every job in our nation is connected in some way to our natural resources. Concern about issues relating to these matters is definitely warranted. Motives and strategies should be questioned and proposals from suspect sources must be scrutinized. As an indication of their collective mindset, globalists contend that individual property rights and jobs must give way to save the earth. They have also suggested that families must be limited in size and regulated to control population and protect children. We can be assured that this is just a preview of more odious recommendations to come.

Not surprisingly, environmentalists are adopting New Age religious views. Using the term loosely, scientists have become *mystics* in the pursuit of environmental purity. People of faith are increasingly being portrayed as enemies of the earth. Propagators of international law are consistently anti-Christian, anti-family, and anti-freedom. A "new" religion with occult overtones is subtly being introduced, and, in some cases, reintroduced on a global scale. When more and more signs point to a growing relationship among paganism, nature worship, and the preservation of natural resources, an unsettling feeling descends upon those of us who cherish our religious freedoms.

Private property ownership is viewed by environmentalists as another threat to the earth. The strategies of environmentalists to eliminate private property rights are slowly surfacing from the shadows. Beware of the hidden meaning lurking behind such concepts as public trust, sustainable development, and biodiversity. Implementation of programs or policies with this kind of philosophical bent would have disastrous ramifications to the American way of life.

All of this leads to the fundamental question—can individual freedoms be sustained in the modern world? It is the sincere hope that this book will provide serious fodder for thought and perhaps motivation for concerned citizens to act in positive and constructive ways so that the glory of American autonomy can be fully restored. There is a crucial need for the sweet air of truth concerning these issues to gently flow through homes, schools, churches, businesses, and marketplaces throughout our nation. Those of us who are amply informed and remain steadfastly alert will be prepared to speak out and fight hard to protect our national sovereignty and ultimately preserve our precious freedoms.

One

The Long Tentacles of Treaties

Americans are drowning in a sea of rules and red tape. Over the last several years, regulations have burgeoned at both the state and local levels, and the aftermath is apparent in almost every aspect of our lives. An even greater volume of burdensome laws emanates from the federal bureaucracy. A morass of environmental regulations and building code requirements delays the construction of infrastructure and development projects in both the public and private sectors. In the health care industry, almost as much time is spent on paperwork as on direct treatment of patients. Education and childcare laws are passed presumably with the best interests of our children in mind, but along with their creation come numerous obstacles to establishing innovative day care centers or alternative schools. For proof, ask anyone who has struggled to start a small business. The difficult task of an entrepreneur is made that much harder by the countless roadblocks and bureaucratic machinations that must be managed.

Enmeshed in these seemingly endless entanglements, most Americans are unaware that yet another insidious bureaucracy is quietly emerging. This bureaucracy has the potential and inherent power to affect the life of every individual in our country, and it lacks even the appearance of democratic protections. Astoundingly, it is generating an incredible volume of laws that are originating, not in our own country, but from outside our borders. It is a sphere of global influence operating as international law.

Because international law activity takes place on the global stage, it seems very distant from matters that typically concern most people in their daily lives. International law generally manifests itself in the form of treaties. Most people think that treaties deal exclusively with the relations among nations. Yet the treaties that are being crafted by internationalists deal specifically with some of the most intimate and private details of our existence, including family relationships, public education, and religious beliefs.

Threats to the Family

Among the major issues that most people would agree we need to address as a society is the decline of the American family. However, there is a startling bit of information with which Americans need to become familiar regarding a further threat to the basic family unit. Influential groups from outside our nation's borders are vigorously and openly at work, making plans to exercise control over our children.

Intellectual global elitists want to shape the worldview of the future to correspond with their own perspective; the traditional family is, by necessity, viewed as an obstacle. Activities such as home schooling and parental discretion over instilling values endanger the desired authority of educational programmers. This was reflected in the thoughts of one-world advocate John Goodlad of the University of Washington and Head of the Institute for Educational Renewal. According to Goodlad, "Parents and the general public must be reached. . . . Otherwise, children and youth enrolled in globally-oriented programs may find themselves in conflict with values assumed in the home."[1]

The UN Convention on the Rights of the Child

The UN Convention on the Rights of the Child[2] is a treaty that was signed in 1990 by leaders of more than seventy nations. It involves the relationship of parents with their children and actually sets children's rights in opposition to those of their parents. Alarmingly, it opens the door for extensive governmental intrusion into the confines of the American home.

It is interesting that the Clinton administration proposed a national system of day care which, in fact, is discussed in this UN convention. There is a provision of the convention that allows children to be separated from their parents when it is deemed necessary.[3] This same provision permits parents to maintain personal contact with their children, but not when it is contrary to the children's best interests. We must ask ourselves, who is going to determine these so-called best interests? In fact, the convention provides for a committee of child-rearing experts to make sure that the treaty is followed.[4] In addition, the Convention on the Rights of the Child refers to "competent authorities" who would be allowed to interfere when a child desires to exercise his or her rights in accordance with the treaty.[5] This committee has already been in operation and has reviewed parenting practices in Great Britain. The committee issued a 1995 report critical of the fact that parents were allowed to withdraw children from sex education classes. The report also expressed dissatisfaction over inadequate social spending and parents using corporal punishments. One of the most well known branches of the UN, the United Nations International Children's Emergency Fund (UNICEF), uses an advertisement slogan that proclaims: "UNICEF, because every child is our child." The intent of the slogan is to show that the United Nations is caring and compassionate, but that is overshadowed by the authority embodied in the treaty to influence personal child-rearing practices.

Judge Charles D. Gill of the Connecticut Superior Court is a cofounder of the National Taskforce for Children's Constitutional Rights. Judge Gill was invited to address the UN General Assembly on Earth Day in 1991. In a law review article written by Judge Gill, he asserts that a child has the right to place himself or herself in an alternative family if this is "necessary."[6] While heaping praise on the UN Convention, he points out that the state is the appropriate body to administer children's rights within the home. His writings depict a world in which the government decides when it is appropriate to remove a child from his or her natural parents.

Judge Gill is among a collection of individuals who call themselves children's rights advocates. Yet these people have had only limited success in affecting public law in America. Consequently, the expected shouts of joy were heard when the United Nations created the UN Convention on the Rights of the Child. This is an illustration of how international law is being utilized as the vehicle to accomplish a desired end when previous attempts using traditional means were unsuccessful.

Some Ominous Proposals

Parents will gain little comfort from knowing that the UN has determined the education of their children must include studies of globalism, feminism, radical environmentalism, and multiculturalism. The UN Convention on the Rights of the Child contains provisions that will astound parents and concerned citizens alike. These ideas are remarkable when we consider that the treaty is being pushed by the Children's Defense Fund and other unified activists.

What would parents think if they discovered that they could be prosecuted for monitoring books, magazines, music, or television programs of their children? This convention grants children the "right" to read, listen to, see, or write about content of their own choosing. This effectively removes any rights of parents to censor what goes into their children's formative minds, including obscene, sacrilegious, or anti-American material.[7] The convention also interferes with the ability of parents to raise their children within their chosen religious faith. It grants the child the "right" to choose different religious pursuits than those of the parents.[8] How will this be enforced? We can look forward to something akin to a global family police force knocking on the doors of American households.

Why would the UN Convention on the Rights of the Child obtain endorsements from groups that encourage sexual relations with minors? These despicable organizations seek to promote a child's "right" to engage in sexual activities that have been universally condemned by all cultures. The convention is of particular interest to these groups because of the rights granted to children and the restrictions placed upon parents with respect to their capacity to regulate persons with whom their children associate.[9]

Rejecting traditional principles of parenting, the convention grants these rights and others to children while taking away the ability of parents to use corporal punishment to discipline their children.[10] The convention uses the high-minded platitude of *the best interests of the child* as the primary factor in determining the suitability of any action concerning children.[11] As is typical of the rhetoric of internationalists, this sounds sensible and proper. Yet, one soon discovers who it is that decides what is in the best interests of the child. Once again, it is the omnipresent state.

All nations that become parties to this agreement are obliged to carry out the provisions of the treaty through all legal measures, including legislative, administrative, and any other available means.[12] In the event this treaty is ratified in the U.S., our nation would be obligated to restructure society in accordance with the provisions. The UN declared 1994 as the International Year of the Family.[13] This was an attempt to convince people that governments should design policy to interfere in family matters in order to avoid negative behavior or exploitation within the family. The establishment of global databases was contemplated in order to identify statistical trends of families of the world. This information would be very valuable for UN experts trying to design "proper" regulations for parents and children.[14]

The Education Nightmare

The United Nations Educational Scientific and Cultural Organization (UNESCO), founded in 1945, was the catalyst for the idea of a global version of the National Education Association (NEA). However, the proposed global variation would be more powerful and would have governmental attributes. The notion of a global board of education has always had a certain appeal to the NEA. Likewise, UNESCO has given the idea extensive consideration. With a board of education in place, the UN could legitimately dictate educational policy on a worldwide basis. If this proposition were to become a reality, any local or parental control of the public school curriculum would be lost.

The issue of sex education provides a good example to illustrate this point. The leaders in UNESCO have had great influence on the propagation of sex education in America. The foundation for modern sex education arose from a UNESCO-sponsored convention that occurred in Germany in 1964. The conclusions reached at the convention were that children rarely learn about sex in their own homes, therefore sex education should begin at an early age, and universal sex education is a worthy and necessary goal.[15] A few months after this conference took place, an organization was established in the United States that became the most influential provider of sex education material in the country. The Sex Information and Education Council of the United States (SIECUS) is an organization that masquerades as a benign educational organization, but is, in fact, an advocate of extravagant and licentious sexual practices. It is virulently pro-abortion, pro-homosexuality, and pro-adolescent contraception, and seeks to impose these perspectives on the children of America. According to SIECUS, adolescents should be taught about a sexual orientation that "describes one's erotic, romantic and affectional attraction to the same gender, the opposite gender, or both."[16]

SIECUS states in their guidelines for sex education that children from age five to eight should be taught about sexual intercourse, living together outside marriage, homosexual relationships, divorce, masturbation, and even abortion. SIECUS predictably derides the traditional family organizations as "right wing" and "fear based." The organizations on the SIECUS list of "far right" groups should feel honored to be included in such distinguished company. The list includes the Family Research Council, Eagle Forum, Educational Guidance Institute, Focus on the Family, and the Rutherford Institute.[17]

In another case of manipulation of our educational system, a 1990 conference sponsored by UNESCO in Thailand called the World Conference on Education for All[18] set up the outline for the Goals 2000 legislation that was passed and signed by President Bill Clinton in 1994. Even though the United States has not formally rejoined UNESCO, its influence has been felt in many of our public schools. Under this systematic plan, students are conditioned to be global citizens and to become aware of world issues rather than studying the traditional history of our nation. The multiculturalism and political correctness contained in such classroom materials owe their origin in part to the UNESCO global education proposals that continue to infiltrate many of our schools.

In yet another illustration, Outcome Based Education (OBE), a catch-all term representing insidious educational philosophy and methodology, is making its presence felt in classrooms across the country. It is a concept that sprang directly from the global school board ambitions of UNESCO. In fact, Goals 2000 is literally saturated with OBE principles. Some of the specific individuals in our country who are promoting this dubious educational approach bear some examination in order to reveal their agenda within the context of international law.

The Educational Power Players

Techniques for this style of education are based on behavioral psychology. The proponents of OBE have utilized the theories of Professor Benjamin Bloom. The foundation of OBE, as expressed by Bloom, denies the existence of absolute truths and embraces the notion of relativism.[19] One idea is as good as another. The acquisition of facts is not part of the equation. Students must learn politically correct attitudes. They cannot be promoted until they display those beliefs on the government-approved list. Additionally, the lack of a moral base leaves teachers with the task of modifying thoughts, feelings, and actions to correspond with a replacement system supplied by the educational establishment. Who do you suppose will create this replacement system? The government is delighted to step in, as needed, with the approved version.

One of the school districts that attempted to implement OBE in the 1980s was located in Chicago, Illinois. The district spent approximately $1.5 million over a seven year period. During the entire seven year period, test scores declined, which alarmed the local politicians enough to cancel the program. The beleaguered parents eventually filed a lawsuit for educational malpractice. The school district ultimately gained the unwanted reputation of being the worst system in the nation.[20]

William Spady is the Director of the International Center on Outcome-Based Restructuring. He is a sociologist who is an unapologetic promoter of globalist goals. Spady's worldview encompasses the ideas of "a fragile and vulnerable global environment," "altering economic consumption," and "collective responsibility." He works with the federal government, private foundations, states, and school districts to help them implement OBE programs. Spady proposes getting rid of the bell curve, phasing out grade point averages, eliminating gifted programs, and avoiding memorization of facts.[21]

In 1986 the Carnegie Foundation issued a report outlining a plan to nationalize education. This foundation is a central funding agency for grant money that supports outcome-based education programs and experiments using funds from the Rockefeller Foundation and similar sources. It has funded and directed the activities of the National Center on Education and the Economy, whose Board of Trustees includes David Rockefeller, Ira Magaziner, Mario Cuomo, and Hillary Rodham Clinton.

Former Secretary of Education William J. Bennett expressed it well when he warned his colleagues of the grave implications of OBE for the country.

> The real concern is when those in the education establishment use OBE to (1) eliminate objective measurable criteria (like standardized tests); (2) do away with the traditional subject-based curriculum in favor of an emphasis on things like general skills, attitudes and behaviors; and (3) advance their own radical social agenda. Increasingly, OBE is applied

to the realm of behavior and social attitudes (becoming, in effect, a Trojan Horse for social engineering, an elementary and secondary school version of the kind of "politically correct" thinking that has infected our colleges and universities).[22]

President Clinton proposed national education standards and national testing. The global agenda is being advanced by the portion of the test on values and attitudes. These tests do not measure knowledge, but rather appraise ethics, beliefs, ideals, and views in a suspiciously subjective manner. It is frightening to imagine the vast amount of private information about our children that has already been collected and compiled in computer systems.

Incremental Encroachment through Our Schools

It is no accident that the Constitution expressly avoided granting the control of law involving family issues to the federal government. The founding fathers held a biblical perspective, where the sacredness of the parental function was not a subject for a centralized government grant. The drafters of international treaties and initiatives purporting to deal with the relations of parents and children, and the education of our citizens, view the world situation quite differently. The UN Convention on the Rights of the Child extends its long tentacles and attempts to penetrate the precious relationship between parent and child.

The plan of education for the world necessitates an incremental move away from traditional scholarly activities, moral absolutes, individualism, and patriotism toward an international collectivist mentality. Once parental rights are completely reduced, as the internationalists envision, the traditional family will no longer be the center and anchor of society. The school will become the organ of the state, with new authority to rear children from the cradle through adulthood. We will have students receiving social security, health care, welfare counseling, nutrition, employment assistance, childcare, and a myriad of other services, compliments of their neighborhood schools. If these planned, international proposals are fully implemented, schools will become indoctrination centers for transmitting the ideals of global citizenship. The new educators will instill in our children an international agenda that is simultaneously being instituted throughout the world. We will lose the freedoms and traditions that have made our nation unique, and it will transform America beyond recognition.

Notes

1. Ron Sunseri, *Outcome Based Education: Understanding the Truth about Education Reform* (Sisters, OR: Questar Publishers, 1994), 17-18.

2. United Nations Convention on the Rights of the Child. Concluded at New York, 20 November 1989. Entered into force, 2 September 1990. General Assembly Res 44/25 (Annex), UN GAOR, 44th Session Supplement No. 49, at 166, UN Doc. A/RES/44/49 (1990).

3. Ibid., Article 9.

4. Ibid., Article 43.

5. Ibid., Article 9.

6. The Honorable Charles D. Gill, "Essay on the Status of the American Child, 2000 A.D.: Chattel or Constitutionally Protected Child-Citizen?" *Ohio Northern University Law Review*, Vol. XVII, No. 3, (1991): 578, as quoted by William Norman Grigg, *Freedom on the Altar* (Appleton, WI: American Opinion Publishing, Inc., 1995), 82.

7. United Nations Convention on the Rights of the Child, Article 13.

8. Ibid., Article 14.

9. Ibid., Article 15.

10. Ibid., Article 29.

11. Ibid., Article 3.

12. Ibid., Article 4.

13. United Nations Resolution 44/82 of 9 December 1989.

14. See *Objectives of the International Year of the Family* (New York: United Nation Publications, 1991). See also Bulletin on IYF, *The Family* (New York: United Nations Publications, 1991).

15. Information concerning the International Symposium on Health Education, Sex Education and Education for Home and Family Living held in Hamburg, Germany, is available from UNESCO Education Information Service, http://www.education.unesco.org.

16. SIECUS Fact Sheet. *Gay, Lesbian and Bisexual Adolescents* (New York: SIECUS, 1998).

17. SIECUS Fact Sheet. *The Far Right and Fear-Based Abstinence-Only Programs* (New York: SIECUS, 1998).

18. UNESCO Education Information Service, http://www.education.unesco.org.

19. Peg Luksik and Pamela Hobbs Hoffecker, *Outcome Based Education* (Lafayette, LA: Huntington House, 1995), 20.

20. George N. Schmidt, "Chicago Mastery Reading," *Learning* (November 1982): 37-39. The Chicago Public School District has since worked hard to remedy the situation by returning to the use of traditional educational practices.

21. Luksik and Hoffecker, *Outcome Based Education*, 18-23.

22. "Outcome Based Education," Empower America Issue Briefing, remarks by William J. Bennett on 27 May 1993.

Two

The Founding Fathers' Worst Nightmare

Most Americans possess little knowledge or direct experience with the subject of international law. Those who are somewhat familiar with the designation may understand that it has something to do with foreign policy but think that it has no real relevance to the federal, state, and local laws with which we all must comply. Unfortunately, this is a dangerous misconception. It is becoming increasingly clear that a group of bureaucrats is using the realm and power of international law to meddle in the internal affairs of countries, and the unfortunate result, in our case, is the subtle erosion of basic liberties.

The Changing Philosophy of International Law

How can people succeed in directing and manipulating national systems at an international level? A dramatic change in the philosophy behind the law is a major factor contributing to their accomplishments. It seems as though modern international law has completely embraced globalism, socialism, and collectivism. In textbooks used at the nation's leading law schools, the redistribution of wealth, radical environmentalism, and extreme feminism are advocated. Some examples of distorted works displayed for future international lawyers include: *Towards a New International Economic Order,*[1] which preaches the redistribution of wealth away from the industrialized nations to the Third World; "Global Apartheid,"[2] which compares the industrialized world, primarily the U.S., with South Africa; and "Feminist Approaches to International Law,"[3] which suggests that "we inhabit a world in which men of all nations have used the statist system to establish economic and nationalist priorities to serve male elites."[4]

One recent campaign to more fully control our lives from an international vantage point involves a proposed treaty called the Convention against Sexual Exploitation. A non-governmental

19

organization (NGO) with consulting status at the UN is promoting this treaty idea. (NGOs are discussed in more detail in
Chapter Ten.) The NGO executive director, Kathleen Barry, an
international law professor at Pennsylvania State University, has
compared sexual abuse and prostitution with sexual harassment
in the workplace. She has stated that the purpose of this campaign is to meet the need for "a comprehensive approach and a
global strategy."[5]

The Elastic Constitution

Another shift in legal philosophy that encourages international lawmakers of this mindset is the loose and distorted way
our Constitution has been interpreted in more recent years. We
have witnessed dramatic changes in our laws. These changes have
often occurred without the passage of any bill by our representatives in Congress. Rather, activist judges have actually been creating laws via court decisions that affect such issues as life, death,
religion, and family. This has obviously had an enormous impact
on our society. Despite their powerful influence, the public has
been denied active participation in such decisions through the
voting process since judges are appointed, not elected to the
bench. In addition, accountability on the part of judges is virtually absent, which leaves us with the compelling question: How
then should the Constitution be interpreted?

A time-tested method for interpreting laws created by Congress involves the examination of so-called legislative intent. The
goals and objectives of members of Congress who draft specific
legislation are consulted. In the same manner, prominent legal
scholars such as Robert Bork have insisted that the only reliable
way to interpret the Constitution is to consult the intent of its
authors. If this principle had been invoked by the Supreme Court,
we would not have had the encroachment upon the legislative
function that we have experienced over the last fifty years. Evidently, the founding fathers agreed with Judge Bork. Thomas
Jefferson wrote a letter in 1823 in which he answered the question of how to interpret the Constitution. He recommended that
we "carry ourselves back to the time when the Constitution was
adopted." He cautioned against finding what "meaning may be
squeezed out of the text" and recommended instead that we look
to the intent of those who created the document.[6]

Squeezing the meaning out of the text is exactly what the federal judiciary and the Supreme Court have done in outlawing school prayer and disallowing states from prohibiting abortion. It is this transformation of the Constitution into a pliable instrument to be molded by activist judges that makes treaties so very dangerous.

Using Treaties to Undermine the Constitution

It appears that international bureaucrats want to use treaty power to completely eclipse the Constitution as well as the Declaration of Independence. The belief that treaty law supersedes the Constitution is held by many of the so-called authorities and highly-placed officials in the international legal community. It is their view that treaties are the supreme law of the land, higher than state and federal law, and in the opinion of international legislators, even the U.S. Constitution.[7]

In 1952 John Foster Dulles described this view perfectly in a speech before the American Bar Association in which he said:

> Treaties make international law and also they make domestic law. Under our Constitution, treaties become the supreme law of the land. They are indeed more supreme than ordinary laws, for congressional laws are invalid if they do not conform to the Constitution, whereas treaty laws can override the Constitution . . . they can cut across the rights given the people by their constitutional Bill of Rights.[8]

It is clear by the sheer number of treaties dealing with domestic issues that the current interpretation of the Constitution is viewed by many as containing a gigantic loophole.

The Founding Fathers' Outlook on Government

Before examining how global bureaucrats specifically intend to incrementally exploit this loophole, it is helpful to review how the founding fathers differed in their view of government from those who promote international law. It also gives us a better idea of just how far we have fallen. Thomas Jefferson wished for three things to be written on his epitaph. The first item was the fact that he founded the University of Virginia. The second was that he drafted Virginia's Religious Tolerance Act. The third was that he authored the Declaration of Independence. It is impressive to

see that Jefferson felt these achievements were even more noteworthy than holding the office of President of United States.

The founding fathers had just ended an extremely difficult
war against the corrupt monarchy of George III. Their distaste
for continued status as a ward of Britain, coupled with intense
desire for independence, was expressed forcefully in Thomas
Paine's *Common Sense.*[9] When George Washington's ragtag army
was pushed across New Jersey by the British, hunger and deser-
tion plagued the troops. Washington asked Paine to write something to motivate them. The essays that Paine wrote began with
the famous line: "These are the times that try men's souls."[10]

The founding fathers lived in a world of monarchs and des-
pots. They knew that the infant nation they were setting up had
to do something unique. They had experienced a divine deliverance of biblical proportions. They were, in fact, able scholars of
history and had examined the factors that led previous nations
into misery. The basis for the new kind of government they
envisioned was expressed in the two most important documents
that established our nation: the Declaration of Independence and
the Constitution. When Thomas Jefferson wrote in the Declaration of Independence that the people are "endowed by their
Creator with certain unalienable rights," he was setting forth an
assumption of the source of such rights. Clearly, the founders did
not believe that these rights came from government, but rather
that they were embedded in all people by the gracious and gen-
erous design of our Creator.

The American View versus the International View of Government

The Constitution describes a limited form of government.
Government would be granted only those specific powers delegated to it by the people. This way of thinking is diametrically
opposed to the founding documents of the United Nations. Instead of declaring that any power not specifically set forth is
reserved to individual citizens, the United Nations interprets its
Charter as authorizing it with unlimited powers. In 1952 the UN
World Court said just that. It stated that even though powers
were not expressly provided to the United Nations, they existed
anyway by "necessary implication" due to the duties that the UN
must perform.[11]

The Constitution expresses individual rights consistent with its view of limited government. The words "Congress shall make no law" appear in the very first amendment of the Bill of Rights. This important phrase illustrates the effective restraint placed upon the federal government to prevent it from legislating in areas that impinge upon the inherent rights of the people.

In UN documents, fundamental rights such as freedom of speech, religion, or assembly proceed solely from the state and can be taken away if necessary. Ironically, totalitarian regimes have used similar language in their government documents to consolidate and solidify their own power.

The Founding Fathers' View of International Law

The founding fathers were concerned with strengthening foreign relations with other nations by bolstering the promises of the United States. In order to accomplish this, they granted to the president, with the approval of the Senate, the power to make and enter into treaties. Moreover, they gave this power exclusively to the federal government. This was to prevent individual states from developing their own international policies and undermining a cohesive foreign policy of the nation. Alexander Hamilton viewed treaties as instruments of agreement between nations and not as international pacts designed to impact individuals. He stated, "Treaties . . . are not rules prescribed by the sovereign to the subject, but agreements between sovereign and sovereign."[12] Hamilton added, "The only constitutional exception to the power of making treaties is, that it shall not change the Constitution . . ."[13]

It is clear that the founding fathers did not agree with current international lawmakers since they held the Constitution as superior in law to any treaty. In fact, Jefferson summed up the view of the drafters of the Constitution by asserting that "if the treaty making power is boundless, then we have no Constitution."[14]

The Treaties Themselves

Jefferson's words stand out in stark contrast when we look more deeply into the sheer volume of treaties, conventions, and conferences that have sought to affect the behavior of individuals rather than relations between nation-states. For instance, the

Chemical Weapons Convention was ratified by the Senate in 1997. This treaty was promoted as a ban on chemical weapons. However, those countries that are most inclined to traffic in weapons of mass destruction are not bound by this treaty. The sovereignty of America is relinquished to an international regulatory body with jurisdiction over the internal affairs of the United States. The World Trade Organization (WTO) was a significant part of the General Agreement on Tariffs and Trade (GATT) passed by Congress in 1994. The WTO constitutes a major loss of sovereignty by the United States. Through the WTO, the American people have yielded significant control over the domestic economy to an international body. This treaty, along with the previous one, was opposed by former administrations. Nevertheless, both were favored by the Clinton administration.

The Law of the Sea Treaty turns the resources of the ocean over to an international bureaucracy. It is presently being promoted by the current administration. If ratified, this treaty would place the economic, industrial, and political activities of seven-tenths of the planet's surface under the control of an international commission. The 1992 Convention on Biological Diversity sets aside significant areas of the country for extremely limited use. If this treaty is ratified, Americans would find their property rights being regulated by an international body. The Clinton administration signed the treaty. Fortunately, however, an attempt to ratify it failed. Arrogantly, the administration forged ahead and implemented part of this UN plan despite rejection by the Senate.

The Climate Control Treaty that was signed in 1997 in Kyoto, Japan, is a further attack on the lifestyle, liberties, and economy of America. This treaty requires the United States to reduce greenhouse gases seven percent below our 1990 levels. China, Mexico, and other developing countries are exempt from the requirements of the treaty. Europe is in a position to comply more easily than the U.S., due to an ample use of nuclear power in that region of the world. The treaty provides for "appropriate and effective" methods of enforcement. To satisfy the Kyoto agreement, the United States will need to restrain its greenhouse emissions by about one-third in comparison with the levels that would otherwise prevail in 2012 by using a third less oil and coal. This will result in dramatic loss of industry, jobs, and choice of transportation in the United States.

Americans traveling the country have been shocked to discover that the UN has claimed many cherished U.S. sites under the World Heritage Convention of 1972. This treaty gives power to the UN to name selected sites in our nation as "World Heritage Sites." Rules affecting the use of these sites will be created at an international level. Believe it or not, these sites include Yosemite National Park, Yellowstone National Park, the Grand Canyon, Independence Hall, and even the Statue of Liberty.

The United Nations Convention on the Elimination of All Forms of Discrimination against Women is typical of the nomenclature used by international drafters. The idea of abolishing discrimination against women is a positive one. However, is it proper to regulate relationships between men and women via international dictates of the United Nations? This treaty has provisions that would change textbooks and other materials used in schools to conform with worldwide political correctness. The United Nations Convention on the Rights of the Child also reaches into the home and interferes with the rights of parents to raise their children. (This treaty was described in Chapter One.)

To Quorum or Not to Quorum

An additional abuse of the treaty power should be observed. The Constitution grants the President power to enter into treaties with the two-thirds approval from the Senate present at the time the treaty is considered. Yet, the Constitution requires a quorum of members in order to legitimately conduct business. It defines a quorum as "a majority of the members." Therefore, in order to approve a new treaty in the Senate, at least fifty-one members should be present. As the following example illustrates, this express regulation is sometimes ignored in the task of ratifying new treaties. A document of the United Nations, the International Covenant on Civil and Political Rights, contains provisions that reach deep into the private lives of American citizens. This treaty was ratified by the United States Senate on 3 April 1992, late in the evening, with only a few senators in attendance. The Congressional record indicates that only five senators were present during this ratification. Conducting the proceedings was majority leader George Mitchell. Mitchell made the motion to approve the International Covenant on Civil and Political Rights, another senator seconded the motion, and the chair, Jay

Rockefeller, called for a vote. Rockefeller requested a vote from the many empty chairs that were present. At that point, he asked if there were any in opposition. With no opposition noted, he announced that the treaty was ratified, and it was made a part of the law of the United States of America. This was done in the name of all Americans.[15]

A Corrupted Application

Because this covenant is now an integral part of the body of federal law in this country, it sits on the books like a trap ready to be sprung. In fact, the trap has already been launched in other parts of the world. In a province of Australia, a group of homosexuals petitioned to overturn a statute that outlawed sodomy. The law that they relied upon was not a domestic law but was none other than the International Covenant of Civil and Political Rights of the United Nations. To the satisfaction of the global bureaucrats, the statute outlawing sodomy in Australia was removed from the books.

In America, international lawyers from outside of this country have suggested orally and in writing that scheduled executions in states like Texas violate this United Nations covenant. Law journals, written to train and share information on criminal defense, have encouraged lawyers to become familiar with the International Covenant on Civil and Political Rights and utilize it in their criminal defense work. A UN inspection team has even visited the United States to conduct investigations of alleged human rights violations in our practice of executing criminals. Predictably, the team decided that our use and implementation of capital punishment violates the laws governing international human rights. A trend is progressing to elevate this covenant so that it will in practice become the supreme law of the land, even to the detriment of our traditional founding documents.

Counterfeit Conferences

International bureaucrats develop ideas regarding future treaties and policies for global-oriented domestic legislation at UN conferences. These conferences are not what they appear to be. The facade at these gatherings is that of free discussion and representation from all parts of the world, with participants seeking to reach mutually agreeable terms on issues. However, long before the respective conferences convene, conclusions have already been decided. The promoters of the conferences draft materials designed to create the concurrence that is ultimately reached. Some of the most notable conferences include the UN Earth Summit held in Rio in 1992, which produced drafts of the Biodiversity Treaty and Climate Change Treaty and assaulted property and economic rights through its so-called consensus. The UN International Conference on Population and Development held in Cairo in 1994 was dedicated to "population stabilization." It became a showcase of ideas for fringe, radical feminism, including the notion that people should be thought of as resources whose numbers must be managed by overseers at the international level. These extreme feminist concepts were extrapolated in a contrived accord in Beijing in September 1995, at the UN Fourth World Conference on Women.

In 1996 the Istanbul Habitat Conference reached an "agreement" that the citizens of the United States should provide housing for the rest of the world. Likewise, the Conference on Food held in Rome in 1996 concluded that the United States should feed all those who hunger in the world. The propositions set forth in these conferences are consistently opposed to traditional values and the free market system. Underlying all of these proposals is the belief that the American standard of living and lifestyle should be drastically modified, and that our wealth should be redistributed throughout the world.

Dangerous Implications

Conferences such as these, and the treaties they generate, constitute a slow, incremental, and deliberate assault on the fundamental principles that our founding fathers prayerfully created. The international legal landscape is now littered with bureaucracies that have the potential to exert tremendous power over our domestic life. Rather than focusing on relations between sovereign nations, these new and proposed bureaucracies aim to dramatically affect our property, our schools, our jobs, and our families. These international legal activities are a direct threat to American life. The loose and flexible treatment of the Constitution by the courts, combined with the view that treaties are the supreme law of the land, are particularly menacing considering the invidious proposals that treaties and conferences embrace.

America is unique among the nations of the world. The ideas set forth in our founding documents stand out in contrast to any other government in history. Consequently, American sovereignty is more than mere nationalism. It is the vessel that cradles the blessings of liberty and so inspires our nation to greatness.

Notes

1. Mohammed Bedjaoui, *Towards a New International Economic Order* (New York: Holmes & Meier, 1979).

2. Gernot Kohler, "Global Apartheid," *Alternatives-A Journal of World Policy* 4 (1978): 263-267.

3. Hilary Charlesworth, Christine Chinken, and Shelley Wright, "Feminist Approaches to International Law," *American Journal of International Law* 85 (1991): 613-29.

4. Ibid., 613.

5. Elizabeth F. Defeis, *Treaties,* International Law Video Course 3, Seton Hall University School of Law (Primos, PA: WTL Distribution, 1995).

6. Thomas Jefferson. Letter to Justice William Johnson, 12 June 1823, *The Jeffersonian Encyclopedia* (New York: Funk & Wagnals, 1900), 209.

7. See William R. Slomanson, *Fundamental Perspectives on International Law* 2d ed. (St. Paul, MN: West Publishing Company, 1995), 341-43.

8. Secretary of State John Foster Dulles, "Treatymaking and National Unity," an address delivered at the regional meeting of the American Bar Association, Louisville, KY, 11 April 1952, as recorded in *Treaties and Executive Agreements,* hearings on S.J. Res. 1 and S.J. Res. 43; Feb., Mar., and Apr. 1953, Y4.J89/2: T71/2, p. 862 and as quoted in William F. Jasper, *Global Tyranny . . . Step by Step* (Appleton, WI: Western Islands, 1992), 101.

9. Thomas Paine, *Common Sense* (New York: Dover Publications, 1997). Originally published in January of 1776 in Philadelphia, PA.

10. Ibid.

11. G. Edward Griffin, *The Fearful Master* (Belmont, MA: Western Islands, 1964).

12. Alexander Hamilton, "The Treaty-Making Power of the President," in *The Federalist* 194, in Richard B. Morris, ed., *Alexander Hamilton and the Founding of the Nation* (New York: The Dial Press, 1957), 193-196. (When the organizers of emerging nations in Eastern Europe and other parts of the world sought to create constitutions for their new found freedoms, they looked to the thoughts contained in *The Federalist Papers*. Unfortunately, the justices who sit on the appellate courts of the United States generally fail to utilize the valuable legacy of the framers' own words.)

13. Alexander Hamilton, "Camillus," No. 36. Draft in Hamilton's hand. Hamilton Papers, 1st ser., 203, in Richard B. Morris, ed., *Alexander Hamilton and the Founding of the Nation* (New York: The Dial Press, 1957), 202-204.

14. Thomas Jefferson. Letter to Wilson C. Nicholas, September 1803, *The Jeffersonian Encyclopedia* (New York: Funk & Wagnals, 1900), 90.

15. The Congressional Record of 3 April 1994 indicates that five senators were present at that evening session. However, a videotape recording of the session showed that the three senators identified were the only ones present according to an audio recording of a speech made by John F. McManus on 28 October 1995 in Orange, California.

Three

The Roots of
International Feminism

Feminism in its most extreme form fits quite comfortably within the spectrum of international treaties, conventions, and conferences. This is due in part to the predominance of a socialist ideology that is shared by many who hold positions of power in international lawmaking. Over the years, feminism has been so closely aligned with Marxism that feminist writers have described the two doctrinal systems as being one and the same. Many women who are currently involved in some of the more extreme feminist movements were associated with Marxist-inspired groups when they were in their youth. Later, when they left these groups, numerous activists utilized Marxist theory to address the political situation of women in a capitalistic society.

From the perspective of many feminists, capitalism is a completely male dominated system reflecting man's fundamental, patriarchal nature. In fact, the true ideologues view the feminist struggle as involving many "evil systems" such as capitalism, that must ultimately be overcome. However, feminists differ from pure Marxists because their goals reach much further than mere class struggles. Where socialist and communist organizers attempt to impose economic standards, radical feminists want to control matters that touch us in a deeper way, extending their influence beyond simply the free enterprise system. Much like extreme environmentalists, feminists such as these wish to implement drastic modifications in our personal lives.

The Gender Agenda

Rejecting any evidence that demonstrates gender differences have a biological basis, feminist activists oppose using gender as a principle of social order. This brand of feminism considers it inherently sexist to use gender in any manner whatsoever to organize society. Any sex role differentiation is viewed as a method by which certain human beings oppress others. Instead, they envision a new kind of society that completely transforms the relationships among men, women, and children so that there is conformance to the feminist ideology rather than letting what is natural or historically customary dictate family relations.

How does a movement go about profoundly changing these most intimate of relationships in a society? The radical feminist answer appears to be through the use of governmental bureaucracy. Moreover, if the goals of feminism cannot be accomplished at the local, state, or national level, a new source of government can be appropriated, that being the powerful, yet accessible, international realm of government.

The feminist movement suffered a severe defeat in 1982 when the Equal Rights Amendment faded into oblivion. However, feminist activists found a new, exciting international playground where they could nurture and develop their ideas. At the international level, they need not be concerned about the restrictions of the Constitution or the Bill of Rights. They found a new way to impose their vision by using United Nations treaties. Thus, the United Nations Convention on the Elimination of All Forms of Discrimination against Women (CEDAW)[1] was born.

International Feminism in New York

The United Nations Convention on the Elimination of All Forms of Discrimination against Women was held in New York in 1979. The convention entered into force in September 1981. It has been accepted by 139 countries. This treaty is often described as an international bill of rights for women. It consists of a preamble and thirty articles that define discrimination against women and regulate what nations must do to end such discrimination. The convention includes a laundry list of potential forms of discrimination without limits as to the type of regulation. It includes any discrimination taking place in "the political, economic, social, cultural, civil, or any other field."[2]

As a participating party of the convention, a nation commits to undertake a series of steps to accomplish the goals of the treaty, which include changing domestic legislation that is incompatible and establishing tribunals and other public institutions to ensure compliance with the treaty. A nation that ratifies the treaty is not only legally bound to put all of the provisions into practice, it is also required to submit a national report at least once every four years on the measures it has taken to comply with treaty obligations. An international bureau with oversight authority was also established to oversee the entire regulatory scheme.

Tragically, this convention is an express interference with the domestic law of the United States and an encroachment on American sovereignty. The use of overly broad language contained in the treaty allows the UN to invade the most personal of relationships between men and women on a number of levels and in a plethora of ways. Our basic, private customs and practices would be subject to international scrutiny. If the United States becomes a party to this treaty, the conduct of men and women in social settings would have to be modified in a legal sense if the international bureau required it. Presumably, our literature, art, and media would be affected. Furthermore, educational materials including textbooks, handouts, and tests would have to adhere to the treaty.[3]

One naturally has to wonder why this particular aspect of societal activity would be the subject of treaties between sovereign nations in the first place. It is true that early in its history international law was confined to matters such as war, peace, and territorial disputes between nations. However, as legitimate concerns surrounding the subject of human rights approached the international level, the door was opened to another agenda—the use of human rights abuses as a pretext to legislate internationally what could not be achieved domestically.

An example of an area of the law that has been a hallmark of state sovereignty in the United States is family law. Marriage, divorce, adoption, child custody, and the like have always been considered the exclusive province of the states. Today, with a significant degree of controversy over such issues as single parent adoption, homosexual marriage, surrogate births, and other atypical family issues, states are jealously guarding their jurisdiction over these matters. The Convention on the Elimination of All Forms of Discrimination against Women would radically change the equation. It would require the states to relinquish their sovereignty over family law entirely.[4] The federal government would appropriate all family law. This would result in the establishment of exclusive federal jurisdiction over marriage, divorce, adoption, and child custody. The federal government would operate under the all-seeing eye of the international bureau created to monitor compliance with the treaty.[5] Despite the fact that this treaty was successfully opposed by previous administrations, the Clinton administration continues to seek its ratification.

UN Conferences Are Not What They Seem

Typically, UN conferences are ten to twelve days long. They commonly have over one hundred different countries represented, with some countries sending twenty or more individuals. With the media and politicians, these conferences sometimes have tens of thousands of people.

UN conferences are yet another means utilized by the globalist community to promote international law. These conferences have the appearance of being democratic gatherings of delegates from all over the globe where input is obtained from all participants. There is an illusion that a consensus among disparate nations is somehow reached in the process, and documents are drafted as a result. This is merely a public relations ploy. In reality, the organizers of the respective conferences write the documentation prior to the start of the event. The delegates are then indoctrinated with the organizers' agenda, resulting in the appearance of consensus through deliberation.

Bella Abzug

Bella Abzug was elected to Congress on a platform of women's rights. She worked as a labor lawyer, peace activist, lecturer, news commentator, and civil liberties advocate, besides being a U.S. representative. She co-founded the National Women's Political Caucus. She cast one of the first votes for the Equal Rights Amendment. On 31 March 1998, Bella Abzug passed away at age seventy-seven.

Ms. Abzug led the Women's Environment and Development Organization (WEDO). Through WEDO she dominated the agenda of UN conferences in order to manipulate affairs and promote conformance to her form of feminism. WEDO is a global organization that actively works to promulgate feminist themes in public policy-making through regional and national advocacy at the United Nations, as well as through international financial institutions. It has been widely recognized as effective in

building coalitions among relevant non-governmental organizations at the UN, as evidenced by the exponential growth of their
influence on official international policy. WEDO's agenda includes changing the economic policies of the World Bank, the
International Monetary Fund, and the World Trade Organization to promote radical feminist ideas internationally. WEDO
has used UN agreements and conventions, and additional agreements and precedents, by uniting sympathetic constituencies.
WEDO has been dominant at the 1992 UN Conference on
Environment and Development (Earth Summit), Rio de Janeiro;
1993 World Conference on Human Rights, Vienna; 1994 Conference on the Sustainable Development of Small Island States,
Barbados; 1994 International Conference on Population and Development (ICPD), Cairo; 1995 World Summit on Social Development (Social Summit), Copenhagen; 1995 UN Fourth
World Conference on Women, Beijing; 1996 UN Conference
on Human Settlements (Habitat II), Istanbul; 1996 World Congress against Commercial Sexual Exploitation of Children,
Stockholm; 1996 UN World Food Summit, Rome; and 1996
First World Trade Organization Meeting of Ministers, Singapore.[6]
Ms. Abzug, in fact, captured control of the conference in Cairo,
Egypt. Together with her organization, WEDO, she changed
the focus from a legitimate discussion of issues to the promotion
of a feminist platform.

Covert Actions in Cairo

In 1994 the United Nations held the International Conference on Population and Development (ICPD) in Cairo, Egypt.
Prior to the scheduling of this conference, it became increasingly
clear that the underlying objective of the organizers was to create
legalized abortion on demand throughout the world. Except for
the action of a few stalwart pro-life advocates, the organizers
would have completely succeeded in their nefarious scheme. The
documents that were drafted at the Cairo conference cleverly
concealed a covert agenda. The pro-life forces disclosed the real
effects that these international documents would have, and many
countries were alerted to the hidden intentions. If these nations
had acquiesced and become a party to the UN documents produced at Cairo, they would have unwittingly created legalized
abortion in their home countries.

The leader of the United States delegation to the Cairo conference was Timothy Wirth, the Under Secretary of State for Global Affairs. One of the themes of the Cairo conference was the empowerment of women. However, the empowerment sought at the Cairo conference referred primarily to the right to birth control and abortion. This so-called empowerment adds authority to the government at the expense of individual moral autonomy.

Changing the Meaning of Words

As is typical of these United Nations conferences, words that are used by attendees may not have the same meaning that the average person would normally associate with them. For example, to most of us, the word *family* refers to a father, a mother, and perhaps some children. To the organizers of United Nations conferences, a family can refer to any arrangement of people who wish to cohabitate for a while. Other terms such as *safe motherhood, family planning,* and *reproductive health* are international euphemisms for abortion on demand. Many of the delegates attending these conferences are not aware of this semantic trickery. The few pro-life advocates who attended the Cairo conference were able to explain the true significance of some of the murky UN terminology. This allowed some nations to opt out of portions of the final document.

The 1992 United Nations Conference on Environment and Development (UNCED), also known as the Rio Earth Summit, was held in Rio de Janeiro. It was the first time the term *sustainable development* gained prominence. Sustainable development is another one of those phrases that cannot be defined by normal custom and usage. One has to examine the meaning of the expression in light of the endless volumes of UN documents that define it. When international bureaucrats use the term sustainable development, they mean that an international regulatory body must control the economic and social activities of people so that the earth's future will be maintained and supported. In more practical terms, this translates into the furtherance of plain, old-fashioned totalitarianism.

The thought process is that with the combination of environmental and population crises, someone or something must save man from himself. Of course, who would know better how to manage the earth than the international bureaucrats? They seriously want to control our future, believing such notions as the earth will run out of food or water if people have too many children, or the polar ice caps will melt if motorists continue to drive pick-up trucks. The idea that people might voluntarily decide to act in responsible ways or devise innovative solutions to address pressing problems never enters their minds.

"Women's health" is another term often heard at United Nations gatherings. In common usage, it sounds as though the phrase refers to the general health needs of women. However, international bureaucrats believe that they can best determine what women require in order to be healthy. Once again, population control appears to be the answer. The UN finds it particularly effective to manipulate Third World nations by aligning the World Bank with organizations such as International Planned Parenthood Federation to coerce Third World countries into legalizing abortion. The bottom line is that developing countries need bank loans. Nothing is more convincing than the allure of money in inducing developing nations to legalize abortion and engage in UN population control programs.

The Beijing Conference

One of four major UN-sponsored conferences that were held in the short span of three years was the 1995 UN Fourth World Conference on Women in Beijing, China. The conference was intended to promote huge social changes. About six thousand delegates attended the actual conference, with approximately twenty-four thousand additional delegates attending a non-governmental organization (NGO) forum. At the last minute, the government of China shifted the NGO meeting to a distant Beijing suburb. The Chinese government would not allow any groups representing Taiwan or Tibet to participate. Visas were refused to several thousand women because their views did not fit with the radical agenda of this UN conference. The government of China wanted to keep the large population of NGOs from being anywhere near the major conference to avoid any lobbying of delegates.[7]

Delegates adopted the Platform for Action and Beijing Declaration. More than sixty delegations commented and more than half submitted formal reservations to sections, including those segments on sexual and reproductive rights, abortion laws, and women's equal right to inheritance. Only those women who were handpicked and screened by the Chinese government were allowed into the women's Beijing conference. The women of China who are genuinely suffering abuse in a most profound manner were not allowed to participate in any part of the conference. It is appalling to realize that many Chinese women have been taken against their will and forced to have abortions. Some women have been locked in detention cells or placed in front of mass rallies to manipulate them into consenting to abortions. Pregnant women have been abducted on the streets and taken, sometimes in handcuffs, to abortion clinics. Women have been captured, tied with ropes, and sometimes placed in large, sealed baskets on these forced journeys to abortion clinics. Female babies, who are perceived to be less desirable, have been butchered, drowned, and left to die. Astoundingly, according to the United Nations, these acts of cruelty do not qualify as interference with the rights of women![8]

Family Redefined

Also at the UN Beijing conference, the government of Canada provided the following statement to define the word *family:* A family is a basic unit of society that comes in diverse and various forms. During the debate, the real purpose for the change of definition emerged. The objective was to promote acceptance of homosexual unions and to suggest that such unions constitute a family. At international conferences, feminists are increasingly characterizing homosexual rights as integral to women's rights. They contend that any type of forced conformity to heterosexuality is an offense against the rights of women. By adopting lesbian rights as their favorite project, feminists can shove homophobia into the vocabulary of feminism.

Bella's Influence

Bella Abzug was very satisfied with the proposals that came out of the Beijing women's conference. She described the platform of the conference as "the strongest statement of consensus on women's equality, empowerment, and justice ever produced by governments."[9] Ms. Abzug was honest in describing conferences such as these as produced by governments. It was, in fact, a blatant example of global governance as described in the *Report of the Commission on Global Governance*.[10] She also indicated the broad application of the ideas generated at the Beijing conference when she said, "We are bringing women into politics to change the nature of politics, to change the vision, to change the institutions."[11]

In the speech Abzug made to the Rio+5 Forum in March 1997, in accordance with WEDO, she portrayed the international activists' view of feminism as encompassing the whole gamut of collectivist thought. She said:

> Thousands of women who organized, as part of the long march to Beijing, to scale the great wall of gender apartheid, shared a common vision. All issues are women's issues. Nothing is separate or off the table. And the values in this vision are now pretty much the same ones that are embedded in the draft Earth Charter. A vision that cares deeply about all people, all creatures, all life on the planet. Some call this an eco-feminist vision. Some call it a spiritual and humanist vision. Some call it a radical feminist vision. Some call it a transformational vision. I call it possible.[12]

There is no question that women are entitled to equal protection under our laws. Constitutional provisions are not meant to apply to a single gender. However, the traditions that we hold dear must not be distorted and corrupted by lawmakers from abroad who are trying to use feminism as a pretext to subvert our system. Furthermore, the institute of marriage requires regulation at a local, rather than a national or international level. The relationship between a man and a woman is still revered enough in our culture that we will not allow it to be the subject of an international experiment in social engineering.

Notes

1. United Nations Convention on the Elimination of All Forms of Discrimination against Women. Concluded at New York, 18 December 1979. Entered into force, 3 September 1981. 1249 U.N.T.S. 13: 1989 U.K.T.S. 2, 1982 Misc. 1, Cm. 643, Cmnd. 8444.

2. Ibid., Preamble.

3. Ibid., Article 5.

4. Ibid., Article 16.

5. Ibid., Article 17.

6. Women's Environment and Development Organization, 355 Lexington Avenue, 3rd Floor, New York, New York 10017. Gopher: gopher://gopher.igc.apc.org/11/orgs/wedo.

7. Kathy Wilhelm, "Women Arrive in Beijing with Hopes for Progress," *The Detroit News* (29 August 1995).

8. Jacqueline Kasun, *The War Against Population: The Economics and Ideology of Population Control* (San Francisco: Ignatius Press, 1988). See also Elizabeth Croll, et al., *China's One-Child Policy* (New York: St. Martin's Press, 1985).

9. Bella Abzug, speech to Rio+5 Forum, 13 March 1997. Women's Environment and Development Organization Archive, 355 Lexington Avenue, 3rd Floor, New York, New York 10017 USA. http://www.wedo.org/.Gopher:gopher://gopher.igc.apc.org/11/orgs/wedo.

10. The Commission on Global Governance, *Our Global Neighborhood: The Report of the Commission on Global Governance* (New York: Oxford University Press, 1995).

11. Fourth World Conference on Women, Plenary Speech given by Bella Abzug as co-chair of Women's Environment and Development Organization in Beijing, China, on 12 September 1995. UN Gopher: gopher://gopher.undp.org:70/00/unconfs/women/conf/ngo/13174219.

12. Bella Abzug speech to Rio+5 Forum on 13 March 1997, United Nations Conference on Women, Women's Environment and Development Organization. http://www.ecouncil.ac.cr/rio5/mar13/abzugen.html.

Four

The First Collision:
The Bird Murders

Ever since the Articles of Confederation were replaced by federalism, a tension has existed over state versus federal power. The desire to be free from a central, dominant, federal government led the leaders of the newly-formed nation to seek to preserve state autonomy, but efforts to undermine the power structure of state governments were at work. The same forces are operating today on the international stage in an attempt to attack and diminish the power of states and the citizens who reside in them.

The Origin of State Sovereignty

The original thirteen colonies were established by separate charters from the English Crown. The only unity among the colonies was their dependence on a common mother country. Each colony had its own governor, legislature, and courts. Additionally, each was governed separately and independently by the English Parliament. Due to parliamentary acts adopted in the late 1760s and early 1770s, political connections between the separate colonies and the English Crown and Parliament deteriorated. In October 1774 the First Continental Congress submitted a petition of grievances to the British Parliament and Crown. They did not mince words. The declaration was drafted with language that pointed out the unjust nature of the acts and described them as an attempt to enslave the colonies. The seeds of revolution had been sown.

During the next two years, the colonies gradually severed relations with England. It took until July 1776 for all traces of British authority to be removed. The formal expression of complete disconnection of the colonies from Britain was contained in the Declaration of Independence. During the period immediately following the Declaration of Independence, the former colonies became independent sovereign states.[1]

> This opinion is predicated upon a principle which is believed to be undeniable, that the several states which composed this Union, so far at least as regarded their municipal regulations, became entitled, from the time when they declared themselves independent, to all the rights and powers of sovereign states, and that they did not derive them from concessions made by the British king.[2]

Each state was the equivalent of a distinct, independent nation. It was only natural that the former colonies would endeavor to organize some framework for unity. The first attempt at such a framework came with the adoption of the Articles of Confederation. Still, state sovereignty remained in the same independent and preeminent status, so much so, that the government of the United States lacked enough central power to be effective. In May 1787 representatives assembled in Philadelphia to attend the Constitutional Convention. After much discussion, a compromise was achieved that improved the viability of the federal government while preserving the sovereignty of the states. When the final version of the Constitution was completed, powers were distributed between the federal government and the states. The founding fathers had witnessed the British Parliament gradually expand its jurisdiction until its own power was virtually unlimited. The framers sought to prevent Congress from usurping powers reserved to the states. In order to provide some protection from this possibility, the federal government was granted only those powers explicitly enumerated in the Constitution.

The Constitution grants no authority whatsoever to the federal government to rule on matters not explicitly delegated. The framers incorporated this premise in the Bill of Rights by reiterating the following in the Tenth Amendment: "The powers not delegated to the United States by the Constitution . . . are reserved to the states respectively, or to the people."

State Sovereignty: A Target of Attack

Over the years, the power of our national government has continued to increase. The courts have played a key role in en-

larging the powers of the federal government at the expense of
state sovereignty. One of the primary tools used today to develop
comprehensive federal schemes is international law. The goal is
to perforate any impediment to change for even the most locally
oriented domestic policy.

Using international law to produce change in domestic policy
is nothing new. In fact, current world conventions such as the
Rio Summit are actually the end result of a belief that domestic
matters can be altered if an initiative happens to originate legally
at the international level. The present flurry of activity on the
international stage has evolved almost through accidental discovery. Issues surrounding the environment provide a vivid example
of influence by circumvention. To understand the reasoning and
agenda behind the approach of environmental activists, it helps
to know a bit about the roots of the movement's infatuation with
the treaty process.

A constitutional justification must exist for the federal government to intervene at the state or local level. When justification is present, federal law is applied in a state, county, or municipal setting. Lawyers commonly refer to this as "federal municipal law." Regulation of the environment has traditionally been
viewed as something that should be handled by individual states
and localities.[3] Since federal municipal law only applies to those
specific areas that are subject to the jurisdiction of the United
States government, absent a specific constitutional justification,
environmental laws should have remained within the exclusive
province of the states. As we shall see, the desire of early environmentalists to prevent the murder of birds that they deemed
needed protection led to the attempted expansion of governmental power into the states' exclusive territory.

The Death of the First Bird

In 1913 Congress passed the Migratory Bird Act[4] which
sought to provide protection to migratory birds by limiting the
hunting season and restricting other aspects of hunting such birds.
Immediately after this act was adopted, federal law officials began enforcement efforts.

In 1914 Harvey Shauver was on a hunting trip to the woods
of Arkansas when he was arrested for shooting the wrong birds.
Unfortunately, the wild prey that Shauver had chosen to hunt

were protected migratory birds. Shauver was indicted, and his lawyer came up with a rather unique defense. The lawyer argued that the Migratory Bird Act violated the Tenth Amendment of the U.S. Constitution. Since historically the regulation of bird hunting was reserved for state lawmakers, the act had illegally trespassed on state sovereignty. Harvey Shauver and his lawyer were elated to hear that Judge Trieber agreed. The judge noted that, according to the common law, states were the owners of birds within their borders. This meant laws that regulated hunting could only come from state legislatures. The judge reasoned that when the constitutionality of legislation is questioned, the court must determine whether or not Congress has the power to pass such a law. If Congress does not have the power, the court must declare the law void. Judge Trieber could not find any authorization for Congress to regulate the hunting of migratory birds in Arkansas, and so he found the Migratory Bird Act unconstitutional.[5]

Putting Their Ducks in a Row

Despite the result in the Shauver case, efforts to enforce the Migratory Bird Act continued. On 2 April 1914 another hunter by the name of George McCullagh went duck hunting during the open season which was permitted by Kansas law. He had a good outing, hitting forty wild ducks. To McCullagh's surprise, he was arrested by Federal Game Warden A.S. Rickner for murdering the feathered friends that were protected by the same congressional legislation. George McCullagh's lawyer thought highly of the result of the Shauver case, so he made the same argument to Judge Pollock that the Migratory Bird Act of 1913 was unconstitutional. Once again, the court agreed. Judge Pollock pointed out that the Constitution grants only those powers to the federal government that are specifically delegated. The judge also stated that there are many matters of law that are lodged in the state, but denied to the nation. (For example, at times, Congress may have wished to control marriage and divorce nationally but did not attempt to do so because these matters are exclusively within the sovereign control of the states.) Judge Pollock said that wild animal and bird life present in a state is the common heritage of all the people of the state. Wildlife should be regulated by the people of the state as they see fit. If the federal government has no property rights concerning these migratory birds, then it has no business enacting laws attempting to regulate them. George McCullagh's indictment was dismissed, and he joined Harvey Shauver as a hunter who had beaten the federal government by effectively utilizing the language contained in the Constitution that limits federal governmental power.[6]

Fleeting Victory

A victory had been obtained for the cause of state sovereignty. Still, those who sought to expand federal power did not give up. They rarely do. State sovereignty had to have an Achilles heel. The protection of all of the poor, defenseless birds required that these government bureaucrats find the vulnerability and exploit it. After a diligent search they discovered a new source of power. It was their hope that through this dominion of authority, they could pierce the shield that state sovereignty provided. It took a couple of years of planning to implement, but in 1916 the United States entered into a new treaty with Great Britain, appropriately called the Migratory Bird Treaty.[7] Two years later, Congress again passed a Migratory Bird Act,[8] but this one was approved in order to fulfill the terms of the treaty.

The federal game wardens were mobilized to enforce the new act. In an amazing case of déjà vu, E.D. Thompson was hunting in Arkansas in 1919. Thompson successfully killed the forbidden migratory birds and was arrested. His case wound up being heard by Judge Trieber, the very same judge who had made the decision for Harvey Shauver. E.D. Thompson's lawyer was no amateur. He had undoubtedly read both the Harvey Shauver and George McCullagh cases, so it was not surprising that he raised the same argument that had prevailed before. If a congressional act regulating birds is beyond the constitutional power of Congress, shouldn't the treaty on the same subject also be beyond constitutional power? Unfortunately, the judge disagreed.

This time, according to Judge Trieber, things were different. Brushing aside the lawyer's analysis, Judge Trieber cited the familiar refrain of Article 6 of the Constitution, which provides that treaties become the "supreme law of the land" and that "every state shall be bound thereby." The judge constantly referred to the fact that the Constitution expressly prevents states from getting involved in treaties with foreign governments. Additionally, the judge reasoned that because treaty power is so important in its relation to other governmental functions of the nation, the result in this case should be different even though the facts were identical. Judge Trieber came to the conclusion that the act passed by Congress fulfilled an obligation assumed by the nation with Great Britain, so E.D. Thompson's indictment would stand.[9] This provided great incentive for those at the international level to use treaties to accomplish what acts of Congress alone could not do.

Adding Insult to Injury

To completely punctuate the internationalists' enthusiasm, less than a month later, in the state of Missouri, George Samples and W.C. DeLapp were both arrested and indicted for successfully hunting, and allegedly murdering protected migratory birds. The attorney general of Missouri entered into the case and tried to restrain the game warden of the United States from arresting or prosecuting anyone hunting wild game within the borders of the state of Missouri. Following almost the exact reasoning as Judge Trieber, Judge Van Valkenburgh decided that treaty power was superior to state constitutions, state laws, and all other state powers, so a congressional act that fulfills the provision of the treaty can invade state sovereignty.[10]

This case ended up going all the way to the Supreme Court of the United States. The Supreme Court heard the argument that had been successful in the Shauver and McCullagh cases: the regulation of wildlife is reserved to the states by the Tenth Amendment and this statute infringed on powers expressly given to the state of Missouri.[11]

It was Supreme Court Justice Holmes who acknowledged that there are limits to treaty-making power. He declared that Congress should not be able to accomplish something by utilizing a treaty that it would be unable to do in absence of a treaty.[12] Rather than use the treaty as a way around state sovereignty, Justice Holmes decided to attack state sovereignty itself.

In order to justify his decision, Justice Holmes first attacked the idea that a state has exclusive authority of title to migratory birds. He stated that this authority is not necessarily exclusive to a state. According to Justice Holmes, wild birds were not in the possession of anyone. Since their presence is temporary, they cannot be considered the property of any state. They are fair game for the federal government to regulate.[13] He then went on to reason that if a treaty is valid, there is no disputing the validity of the congressional law. As long as the treaty and the subsequent law deal with matters of national and international concern, they are proper.[14] Not all of the U.S. Supreme Court Justices agreed. Two of them wrote a dissenting opinion affirming state sovereignty as a valuable element of our form of government.[15]

Expanded Use of Treaties

The opponents of state authority continued to experiment with their new powerful tool. In 1936 a treaty was solidified with Mexico which also created regulations over the hunting of migratory birds. This treaty was even more specific than the one that had been entered into with Great Britain in 1918.[16]

Now that the promoters of this migratory bird protection found that they could penetrate state sovereignty with treaties, they began to see just how deep and pervasive their newfound power was.

In many ways, the original intent of the founding fathers in limiting federal power has been thwarted. State sovereignty has been successfully attacked and local matters have been unduly regulated. One of the greatest threats to individual freedoms comes from the international level. The objective of protecting birds failed to produce the desired results when approached in a conventional way. Nonetheless, an international treaty allowed an invasion into provincial affairs, and so from an unassuming beginning, the use of treaties to create domestic law flourished. As we shall learn, international planners have determined that no corners of our lives should be left ungoverned.

Notes

1. *M'Ilvaine v. Coxe's Lessee*, 8 U.S. (4 Cranch 209, 1808).

2. Ibid., 212.

3. United States Constitution, Article I, Section 8 cl. 17.

4. 37 Stat. 828, 847, c. 145.

5. *United States v. Shauver,* 214 F. 154 (E.D.Ark. 1914).

6. *United States v. McCullagh,* 221 F. 288 (D.Kan.1915).

7. 39 Stat. 1702.

8. Migratory Bird Act of 3 July 1918, 40 Stat. 755, C. 128, U.S. Comp. St. 1918, p. 1795.

9. *United States v. Thompson,* 258 F. 257 (E.D. Ark. 1919).

10. *United States v. Samples,* 258 F. 479 (W.D. Mo. 1919).

11. *Missouri v. Holland,* 252 U.S. 416, 40 S.Ct. 382 (1920).

12. Ibid., 252 U.S. 416, 431-433.

13. Ibid., 252 U.S. 433-435.

14. Ibid., 252 U.S. 435.

15. Ibid.

16. *United States v. Selkirk,* 258 F. 775 (S.D. Tex. 1919).

Five

Coercive Population Control

Emulating the nineteenth century philosopher Hegel, international bureaucrats have been utilizing fear to propel their agenda. Hegel believed that fear was an extremely effective tool in the manipulation of a society. Following Hegelian principles, those who wish to create a new bureaucracy seek to manufacture a crisis. As a result, the public has been bombarded by claims of an overpopulation crisis that threatens to ruin our world. Since human beings cannot possibly survive this apocalyptic future, a regulatory body must emerge at the international level to assert control over the details of our reproduction.

UN History Concerning Reproduction

The United Nations has a long history of promoting stringent population control policies. Back in the late 1940s, the first director general of the United Nations Educational Scientific and Cultural Organization (UNESCO) was Julian Huxley. Huxley was so extreme in his views that he considered radical eugenics, the improvement of the human race by denying selected people the ability to reproduce, as a viable option for UNESCO's use at an unspecified future date. He acknowledged that people generally regard eugenics as unthinkable, but he predicted that those opposed would someday come to see its merits.[1]

Population and family planning have been a part of every United Nations conference since 1967, when UN Secretary General U. Thant promoted a declaration on population. The declaration put forward the notion that fertility control was a human right. This point of view has been particularly prominent at UN conferences on environmental matters.

The Intricate Web of Population Experts

The relationships that exist between international bureaucracies involved in population issues are quite complex and intricately interconnected. For instance, James D. Wolfensohn is the president of the World Bank and also serves on the board of the Population Council of the United Nations. He has let it be known that he is willing to provide the money that is necessary to implement UN population reduction programs. Dr. Fred Sai of Ghana was president of the International Planned Parenthood Federation (IPPF) from 1989 to 1995. During the time that he served as an officer at IPPF, he also worked at the World Bank in a division that was involved with population control activities. When Third World countries looked to the World Bank for help with financial matters, they found that there was a condition attached to obtaining loan assistance. Before countries could receive the desired funding, they were first required to establish population control programs. Since these nations were inexperienced in implementing population control programs, Dr. Sai was ready and able to provide the necessary expertise through his connections to IPPF. Conveniently, the services of IPPF could be used to help these Third World nations adopt "correct" family planning approaches. The same Dr. Sai was also the chairman of the United Nations International Conference on Population and Development (ICPD) held in Cairo, Egypt, in September 1994. At this conference, a resolution was presented that allocated seventeen billion dollars per year for population control.

The Population Control Awards

The United Nations is so obsessed with population control activities that it holds a yearly awards ceremony for those who sell the agenda in the strongest way. This tribute is aptly entitled "The UN Population Award." The honor is bestowed annually on individuals and institutions that make "outstanding contributions to increasing awareness of population problems and their solutions."[2]

In June 1997 a Thai senator, Mechai Viravaidya, was addressing the UN awards ceremony at which he and two other family planning experts were presented with diplomas, gold medals, and a share of the monetary prize of $25,000. Senator Viravaidya said: "In the midst of uncertainty of interpreting the law, it is men who legislate, harass, and arrest, and it is the women who suffer. Our laws deny safe termination of pregnancy

to the women who need it most desperately. We must stop this
hypocrisy."[3]

Early Eugenics with Margaret Sanger

The present day population control agenda has an undistinguished pedigree. Its roots can be traced back to the birth of
Planned Parenthood, and its infamous founder, Margaret Sanger.
In January 1932 Sanger gave an address before the New History
Society in New York. The speech was subsequently published in
an article that summarized Sanger's proposals for the future of
the nation. Among her suggestions was the proposition for the
appointment of a "Parliament of Population" to direct and control the population through birth rates and immigration. This
new governmental agency would

> keep the doors of immigration closed to the entrance of
> certain aliens whose condition is known to be detrimental to
> the stamina of the race, such as feebleminded, idiots, mo-
> rons, insane, syphilitic, epileptic, criminal, professional pros-
> titutes, and others in this class barred by the immigration
> laws of 1924; . . . apply a stern and rigid policy of steriliza-
> tion and segregation to that grade of population whose
> progeny is tainted, or whose inheritance is such that objec-
> tionable traits may be transmitted to offspring; . . . insure
> the country against future burdens of maintenance for nu-
> merous offspring as may be born of feebleminded parents, by
> pensioning all persons with transmissible disease who vol-
> untarily consent to sterilization; . . . give certain dysgenic
> groups in our population their choice of segregation or steril-
> ization; . . . apportion farm lands and homesteads for these
> segregated persons where they would be taught to work
> under competent instructors for the period of their entire
> lives.[4]

Ms. Sanger believed that those determined to be unfit should
not be allowed to reproduce. Her views reflect an insidious underlying philosophy, devoid of any kind of moral conscience. A
purely secular, purely utilitarian view of society such as this ultimately leads to the justification for the disposal of human beings.
In order to promote her agenda, Sanger opened a birth control
clinic in a neighborhood that was mostly populated by newly-

arrived, minority immigrants. The community included people of Italian, Hispanic, and Jewish descent.

In 1939 Sanger created a program designed to eliminate segments of the population that she believed constituted an inferior race, namely, people of black heritage. She had expressed the conviction that black people were of the lowest intelligence and fitness in the entire population. To market her birth control services, she utilized members of the black clergy. Sanger said that black ministers were most successful at convincing their followers of the merits of birth control.[5]

Sanger's writings depict people who are part of religious groups, such as fundamentalists and Catholics, as expendable members of society. She often referred to Christianity as tyrannical and expressed her desire to rid the world of the Christian faith. Not surprisingly, Sanger found an attraction for the teachings of Theosophy (to be discussed in Chapter Eight). The views of Margaret Sanger seem thoroughly extreme to anyone unaccustomed to the ravings of population control advocates. Yet a similar attitude regarding the dispensability of human beings is prevalent today in the international, environmental, and feminist camps.[6]

Petrified of the Population

One of the first population scare campaigns to gain attention was promulgated by Thomas Robert Malthus. In his work, *An Essay on the Principle of Population* (1798), he concludes that poverty and distress are unavoidable because population increases faster than the means of support. Malthus suggested that only war, famine, and disease could check population growth, but later added moral restraint.[7] At the time of its pronouncement, his theory was very controversial. However, despite the devastating consequences anticipated by Mr. Malthus, population levels did not rise to the numbers he expected. Consequently, his name spawned a new word, *Malthusian,* used to describe dire doomsday predictions that do not pan out.

In 1968 another champion of the gloom and doom philosophy, Paul Ehrlich, wrote a book entitled *The Population Bomb.*[8] Ehrlich referred to population growth as a cancer and predicted world calamities if radical measures were not taken immediately.

The radical measures recommended by Ehrlich included abortion, compulsory birth control, and even adding drugs to water supplies so that parts of the population would be rendered impotent. Ehrlich went on to predict that human population would wind up drastically reduced by various catastrophes that would occur prior to the mid-1980s. Ehrlich failed as a prognosticator, but that did not deter him. In a second book written in 1970, he predicted that the increases in population would cause the earth to cool.[9] He has yet to reconcile this forecast with the global warming theories presently in vogue. So the Malthusian refrain rings on as population control advocates raise their voices in an attempt to bolster their cause.

Sanger Goes Global

The United Nations confers non-governmental organization (NGO) status on those groups most closely aligned with the global agenda. A primary example of this is the International Planned Parenthood Federation (IPPF). It is ironic that IPPF has been given status as a non-governmental organization because it would not be able to exist without government subsidies. IPPF applied for NGO status with the Untied Nations in 1955. At that time, opposition by governments with significant Roman Catholic populations lobbied to reject the status for IPPF. By 1964 world attitudes had been manipulated to a sufficient degree that IPPF was successful in its bid. By 1973, when the United Nations held a World Population Conference in Mexico, IPPF had obtained the highest status of any affiliated NGO within the world body.

Pro-life groups have not fared as well. Human Life International, a pro-life organization, had its application for NGO status rejected by the United Nations. The reason given for this rejection was that Human Life International had campaigned against the practice of children in the United States collecting money for UNICEF. However, this was merely a pretext to obscure the real reason for rejection—pro-life groups run counter to the reproductive agenda of the UN. This is apparent when we observe that a pro-choice Roman Catholic group, Catholics for Choice, has been accepted as an NGO.[10]

The World Population Emergency Campaign

The World Population Emergency Campaign (WPEC) is a private organization administered by IPPF. It was set up for the purpose of warning Americans of the urgent danger of the "world population explosion." After instilling sufficient fear, WPEC turned to raising money for international birth control and family planning programs. With the slogan "not just another cause, but the problem of our time," WPEC attempted to publicize the perils of world population growth. Through advertisements in the *New York Times*, meetings with business leaders in various cities, and mass mailings signed by Margaret Sanger and novelist James A. Michener, WPEC raised money for IPPF projects. Money raised by WPEC has been used by such organizations as the Family Planning Association of India to finance a mobile field clinic and the Margaret Sanger Research Bureau in New York City to provide free distribution of birth control literature and devices.

WPEC's largest fund-raising event was the Margaret Sanger World Tribute held in New York City in May 1961. The occasion marked the forty-fifth anniversary of Sanger's opening of the Brownsville Planned Parenthood Clinic. Following this conference was a fund-raising dinner chaired by Julian Huxley. The tribute fund immediately exceeded its $100,000 goal. Margaret Sanger's attendance at this event was her last major public appearance.

IPPF and the Spread of Death

The IPPF consists of national affiliates in over 150 countries worldwide. It was founded in Bombay in 1952 by the leaders of national family planning associations in eight countries. The founding countries were India, Germany, Hong Kong, the Netherlands, Singapore, Sweden, the United Kingdom, and the United States of America. IPPF states in its literature that it seeks "the highest possible level of sexual and reproductive health."[11] However, it constantly ties in world population control in its literature and activities. This organization campaigns locally, regionally, and internationally through politicians and the media to lobby for its agenda.

Not only is IPPF involved with the spread of abortion throughout the world, but it uses aggressive sex education to indoctrinate young people all over the globe. IPPF has consultative status as an NGO at the United Nations. It works with UN agencies, governmental and intergovernmental groups, and private organizations that share its "culture of death" agenda. These organizations include the United Nations Population Fund, the United Nations Children's Fund, the World Health Organization, the World Bank, and many others.

Shaping the Minds of Children

The IPPF has released an international publication called *Mezzo*. Its promotional material indicates that *Mezzo* "equals nothing but the truth about sex."[12] *Mezzo* has published surveys conducted in fifty-four countries. Respondents to the surveys ranged in age from fourteen to twenty-four and were questioned on the subjects of "friendship, love, early marriage, contraception, and pregnancy."[13] *Mezzo* is described as a youth magazine designed to provide information on sexual abuse, homosexuality, abortion, sexually transmitted diseases, and all aspects of sexual relationships for young people. In a July 1997 IPPF press release, *Youth Speak Out On World Population Day*, the results of the above-mentioned survey were discussed. A fourteen year-old boy from New Zealand expressed his view on sexuality in this way: "It's my life, my body, my choice." IPPF touted this disturbing declaration as part of their new survey called *Generation 97*, which was published by the International Planned Parenthood Federation and the United Nations Population Fund.[14] *Generation 97* was released on World Population Day to present the ideas of the young people of the world concerning early marriages, contraception, abortion, pregnancy, and parenthood. IPPF is not satisfied with merely spreading its agenda to adults. It sees the need for pre-adolescents and teenagers to fully explore their sexuality. "Young people have the right to express themselves and the right to make their own decisions. It is our duty to help them realize these rights."[15]

IPPF believes that it is the leader of the family planning movement in the NGO sector of the United Nations. Despite the professed topic of a conference or a convention, population control advocates always try to find a way to tie in their agenda.

At the United Nations Food Summit held in Rome in 1996, IPPF was present to advance its version of reproductive health. Critics may have argued that an international conference on food was not the place for discussion of population control or feminism. However, the secretary general of the International Planned Parenthood Federation, Ingar Brueggemann, made a speech to the UN Negotiating Committee gathering in Rome in preparation for the World Food Summit. She defended her position, stating that "reproductive health is one of the keys to population control, which in turn will reduce the burden on the world's scarce food resources."[16]

Included in the discussion of food and hunger, the documentation produced by this conference contains language on integrating population policies and family planning services into the final paperwork. The term *reproductive health care* was used more often in these documents than any language related to food or hunger. Secretary General Brueggemann also stated that until women have access to reproductive health care, the world food problem could not be solved.[17] Sadly, in international conference language, reproductive health care is just another code for abortion on demand.

Oppression in China

It is beyond most people's capacity to imagine that anyone would promote forced reduction of population. It is even more difficult to believe that the government of a country would work as a population reduction advocate. However, when the inhumane and repressive policies of the government of China are exposed, it quickly destroys any illusions people might hold. China's coercive family planning policy has created a nightmare, all in the name of population control. Chinese authorities have ordered the forced abortion, sterilization, and infanticide of millions of their own people.[18] There have even been reports of the sale of human fetuses in China for medicinal purposes. Children have been tortured, starved, and sexually abused in state orphanages. Women are routinely physically carried off to clinics for abortions of what are considered to be unlawful pregnancies.

China's cultural preference for boys has created skewed numbers when it comes to the gender of children. There are around 118 male births reported for every 100 female births. In some surveys, the numbers run as high as 159 male births for every 100 female births. This is, of course, highly unnatural and cannot be occurring without one of two abominable explanations. Either abortion of female fetuses is responsible for this great discrepancy or female babies are being murdered after they are born. Despite the perpetration of all these atrocities by the Chinese government, it still did not prevent the U.S. government from funding China's population control program. In addition, forced abortions and sterilizations are being done with the assistance of the United Nations Population Fund, which has provided approximately $150 million to Chinese population reduction programs. These practices are totally incongruous with the United Nations conventions, conferences, and international agreements that ostensibly protect human rights.

The Clinton administration restored taxpayer funding for the UN Population Fund. Moreover, the Clinton administration reinterpreted asylum law so that Chinese women who have fled their homeland and come to the United States to save their unborn children from abortion, or themselves from forced sterilization, are classified as criminals. These women are denied asylum, and their legitimate human rights concerns are ignored. In the end, Chinese women seeking asylum are treated like fugitives and delivered back into the hands of the real offenders—Chinese officials.

Human Rights Violations around the Globe

Numerous other violations of human rights in the name of population control were committed against women throughout the world by so-called family planning organizations. During the 1970s, soldiers herded the women in Bangladesh, against their wills, and took them for forced procedures involving the insertion of contraceptive devices. During the next decade, a family planning organization funded by the U.S. misled women in Haiti and Bangladesh about the risks of the controversial abortifascient drug, Norplant. When these women suffered severe health problems from the use of Norplant, extraction of the devices was denied.

Scores of Third World countries implemented strategic sterilization programs with many women sterilized without their consent. There are cases where women were actually refused humanitarian assistance during a disaster until they agreed to be sterilized. Promoters of population control have an appalling track record. In the early 1970s family planning organizations dispensed over 700,000 Dalkon shields to women in the Third World, with the financial support coming from U.S. taxpayers. These Dalkon shields turned out to be unhygienic and dangerous. Thousands of women may have died due to this contraceptive crusade.[19] In Kenya children died from the treatable disease of pneumonia because contraceptives take priority over the much-needed medicines in health clinics. Women in many developing countries must submit to contraceptives before they can receive economic aid or medical treatment.

The internationalists who advocate population control assert that so-called family planning is of paramount importance to people in developing countries. If a survey of the most urgent needs of citizens of Third World countries were taken, it is highly unlikely that a crate of contraceptives would top the list of their most compelling necessities.

Fear is a powerful tool. Dubious apocalyptic predictions have been used for decades to scare the world into the acceptance of previously unthinkable measures. Population control organizations are, in effect, international bodies that influence and legislate at UN conferences and conventions. Taxpayer funds are secretly funneled into coercive population control programs via UN-related agencies. The population control agenda constitutes just one more piece in the international law puzzle that, when assembled, shows a comprehensive attack on national sovereignty.

Notes

1. William Norman Grigg, *Freedom on the Altar* (Appleton, WI: American Opinion Publishing, Inc., 1995), 108.

2. Pro-Life E-News Canada. "Three Population Experts Receive UN Award" (10 June 1997). http://www.interlife.org/.

3. Ibid.

4. Margaret Sanger, "A Plan for Peace," *Birth Control Review* (April 1932): 107-108.

5. Linda Gordon, *Woman's Body, Woman's Right: Birth Control in America* (New York: Penguin, 1990), 64.

6. See Michael Cromartie, Midge Mecter, and Nicholas Eberstadt, *The Nine Lives of Population Control* (Grand Rapids, MI: Eerdmans, 1995).

7. Thomas Robert Malthus, *An Essay on the Principle of Population* (New York: Oxford University Press, 1993).

8. Dr. Paul R. Ehrlich, *The Population Bomb* (New York: Ballantine Books, 1968). See also Paul R. Ehrlich and Ann H. Ehrlich, *The Population Explosion* (New York: Simon & Schuster, 1990).

9. Paul R. Ehrlich and Ann H Ehrlich, *Populations Resources: Issues in Human Ecology* (San Francisco: W.H. Freeman and Company, 1970).

10. From a speech given by Cynthia Bell on 16 April 1997 at the 17th Annual World Conference of Human Life International, Minneapolis, MN.

11. Literature available at IPPF, Regents College, Inter-Circle, Regents Park, London NW1 4NS, UK.

12. From a February 1998 press release from IPPF.

13. Ibid.

14. IPPF news and press release, "Generation 97-Youth Speak Out On World Population Day" (July 1997).

15. Ibid.

16. IPPF news and press release, "IPPF Calls for Strong Support of Rights of Women at Rome Food Summit" (24 October 1996).

17. Ibid.

18. Steven W. Mosher, *China Misperceived: American Illusions and Chinese Reality* (New York: Basic Books, 1992). Steven Mosher became one of the first non-Communist Westerners to be allowed to live in rural China in the 1970s.

19. See Morton Mintz, *At Any Cost: Corporate Greed, Women and the Dalkon Shield* (New York: Pantheon, 1985).

Six

One Senator's Battle

The subject of national sovereignty is not usually a topic of general discussion. Maybe it is because we simply take our sovereignty for granted, or maybe it is because we have not felt an urgency about the issue. In light of some recent occurrences, though, there may be good reason to give this area more of our attention. Why is American sovereignty so important? Why do some people concern themselves with the matter of preserving our nation's sovereignty? The origin of the grand attempt at representative government that we call America was based upon a divinely inspired and unique political perspective. Our nation was founded upon the premise that individual rights do not come from the state but are endowed to us by the Creator. Power is vested in government solely through a legal conveyance from the people. The document our founding fathers used for delegation of this power was the Constitution.

An International Pledge

As we explored earlier, in order to enable the federal government to effectively engage in foreign affairs with other nations, the Constitution provides that treaties shall be the supreme law of the land. The founders never intended to furnish the means for any branch of government to utilize treaties to bypass other constitutional prohibitions. Yet treaties and international agreements have been used more and more frequently to control domestic matters. As this occurred, citizens both within and outside government began to sense the danger that the practice posed to the integrity of the Constitution. One concerned citizen was Senator John Bricker, who in 1952 proposed a constitutional amendment to place clear limitations on the legal applicability of treaties in order to preserve individual and states' rights, as well as American sovereignty.[1]

Uneasiness over the escalating authority of treaty power first surfaced when the United States Supreme Court heard the case of *Oyama v. California* in 1948.[2] The case dealt with a law that had been passed by the state of California called the California Alien Land Law. This controversial statute did not permit certain aliens who were ineligible for citizenship to own land. The language in the concurring opinions written by Justices Black, Murphy, Douglas, and Rutledge expressed a troubling rationale for holding that the law was void. They stated that the law could not be enforced because it conflicted with Article 55 of the United Nations Charter.[3] The United Nations Charter is the founding document of the UN. It was and still is a fully ratified treaty. Article 55 declares that the United States, as a party to the treaty, is legally bound to promote "universal respect for, and observance of, human rights and fundamental freedoms for all without distinction as to race, sex, language, or religion."[4] The concurring opinion reasoned that since this was an international pledge, state laws that bar land ownership by aliens interfere with that international pledge. Basically, a state law was held invalid by using the words of an international UN treaty. We already have protections for human rights and fundamental freedoms contained within our state constitutions and, of course, our federal Constitution's Bill of Rights. Yet, the Supreme Court justices chose to rely on the UN Charter instead of our own documents and laws as a basis for their ruling.

Two years after the *Oyama* case, a California district court in 1950 followed the same reasoning that the Supreme Court had laid down in the *Oyama* decision. This federal trial court again held that the California Alien Land Law was invalid because it violated the provisions of Article 55 of the United Nations Charter and characterized that document as the supreme law of the land.[5] Once more, the UN Charter had profoundly influenced the law of an American state.

In essence, the United Nations Charter had been judicially determined to be the supreme law of the United States. In the aftermath of these two cases, legal scholars began to catalogue numerous state and federal statutes that should be overturned by the UN Charter. In addition, the rationale utilized in *Missouri v. Holland,* mentioned previously in Chapter Four, now became legally significant in that the treaty power could be the foundation for expanded congressional power beyond what is set forth in Article 1, Section 8 of the Constitution.[6]

The Bricker Amendment

Politicians and conscientious citizens were apprehensive about this emerging legal climate. Their nervousness was exacerbated by the imminent approach of the International Covenant on Human Rights of the United Nations that was being prepared by the United Nations Human Rights Commission. Support soon developed for a constitutional amendment to limit the scope of federal treaty power. During 1951 and 1952, the legislatures of Colorado, California, and Georgia petitioned for just such an amendment. The House of Delegates of the American Bar Association (ABA) in February 1952 recommended an amendment to Congress which asserted that if a provision of a treaty conflicts with a provision of the Constitution, it shall not be enforceable. During the same month, Senator John Bricker from Ohio introduced a comprehensive constitutional amendment that followed the ABA's concept. It would soon become known as the Bricker amendment. According to this amendment:

> Section 1: A provision of the treaty which conflicts with this Constitution shall not be of any force and effect; Section 2: A treaty shall become effective as internal law only legislation which would be valid in the absence of a treaty; Section 3: Congress shall have the power to regulate all Executive and other agreements with any foreign power or international organization. All such agreements shall be subject to the limitations imposed on treaties by this article.[7]

It is of particular interest that a provision in the Bricker amendment sought to bring executive agreements under congressional control. The inclusion of this provision stemmed from President Franklin Roosevelt's frequent use of executive agreements in his conduct of foreign relations.[8]

Senator Bricker was merely attempting to repair a growing hole in the constitutional fabric of American government. He sought to restore the proper place of the U.S. Constitution in relation to international law. Under the provisions of the Bricker amendment, the Constitution would have primacy over any treaty that our nation signed with another country or countries or with an international organization. The opponents of the Bricker amendment expressed concern that the amendment would intrude upon the president's power to conduct foreign affairs and would interfere with foreign policy. This has always been the familiar refrain of those who want to expand presidential power despite the provisions of the Constitution.

By January 1953 Senator Bricker was able to state publicly that he had at least sixty-four members of the Senate who promised to sponsor his proposed amendment. It was at this time that the opposition mounted, particularly from the Eisenhower administration. President Eisenhower began a campaign in earnest to defeat the Bricker Amendment, and he assigned the task of waging the fight to his secretary of state, John Foster Dulles. This was the same Mr. Dulles who two years before had emphatically declared that international treaties possess the power to diminish or even eliminate those guarantees granted by the Bill of Rights.[9] In February 1954 the Senate voted sixty to thirty-one in favor of the amendment. However, this was one vote short of the required two-thirds majority needed to approve a modified version of the original Bricker amendment. With this defeat, Bricker's proposal rapidly lost its political force.[10]

The Amendment for American Sovereignty

Today we see an ever-expanding number of treaties, conferences, and covenants that reflect a globalization of our political, economic, and judicial institutions. International initiatives that reduce or eliminate sovereignty, such as the World Trade Organization (WTO), the International Criminal Court, and the Global Warming Treaty, have profound effects at the local, state, and national levels. The United States now faces a much more serious dilemma than the one that prompted Senator Bricker to fight for his amendment. It is clear that many international treaties and agreements manifest a distinct intention to override constitutional protections and thereby compromise U.S. autonomy.

A current member of Congress, Representative Helen Chenoweth of Idaho, has realized the dangers of the present international legal climate and is introducing a modern version of Senator Bricker's amendment. It is called the Amendment for American Sovereignty.[11] Much like its predecessor, the Amendment for American Sovereignty has four basic goals: to elevate the Constitution's primacy as legal authority over any treaty; to deny the enforceability of any treaty provision that would infringe on state legislative authority, unless that provision is ratified by a plurality of state legislatures of the United States; to propose to disallow the jurisdiction of international courts in any American domestic activities; and to provide that no treaty can become effective in the United States without enactment of supporting legislation by Congress.

Ms. Chenoweth has expressed her objectives this way:

> In the past we've rarely worried about our executive binding us in international treaties to laws that are unconstitutional. With the recent broad expansion of powers under the Clinton administration, however, and with the president's increased activities in creating international law, the threat of an international court controlling American domestic policy has become very real. The implications reach into our natural resources, defense, civil rights, and all the other rights that Americans are guaranteed by the Constitution and our Bill of Rights. All stand in jeopardy to international treaties or executive agreements.[12]

In reality, Representative Chenoweth is attempting to ensure that Americans will be governed by laws made by our duly elected representatives and not by directives of treaties, international agreements, or foreign judiciaries. This proposal does not do away with treaties or agreements. It does not interfere with foreign policy or take away the incentive of the United States from developing international relationships.[13] Trying to pass this amendment in both the House of Representatives and the Senate is an uphill battle. Still, the story of the original Bricker amendment needs to be told and retold. A debate on the issues that first prompted Senator Bricker, and now move Representative Chenoweth, to act is urgently needed by the nation.

Sovereignty is a term that refers to the specific, blessed nature of our system of government as expressed by our founders in the documents that constitute the basis of our republic. Representative Chenoweth, and others like her, must be supported so that we can put a halt to the relinquishing of our priceless liberties and, once again, restore authority and dominion to their proper places.

Notes

1. James Hirsen, "Sovereignty 101," *Covenant Syndicate* 1, No. 62 (12 January 1998). http://capo.org/opeds/sov101.html.

2. *Oyama v. California*, 332 U.S. 633 (1948).

3. Charter of the United Nations. Concluded at San Francisco, 26 June 1945. Entered into force, 24 October 1945. Reprinted in 1 Weston I.A.1, Article 55.

4. Ibid.

5. *Fujii v. State*, 217 P.2d 481 (1950).

6. Much legal discussion turns on the question of whether a treaty is, in fact, "self-executing." Courts take the position that if a treaty is not self-executing, then it needs federal legislation, or so-called supporting legislation, before it becomes the supreme law of the land. Using this interpretation, the California Supreme Court upon appeal ruled in *Fujii v. State*, 242 P.2d 617 (1952), that the district court had erred in voiding the California Alien Land Law because the United Nations Charter was not self-executing. However, the court here held that the law was invalid because it violated the Fourteenth Amendment's Equal Protection Clause.

7. United States Senate Joint Resolution 130, 1952.

8. See Chapter 11, "Trading Away the Constitution."

9. See Chapter 2, "The Founding Fathers' Worst Nightmare."

10. The original Bricker amendment had gone down to defeat in the U.S. Senate forty-two to fifty, with four senators not voting. The modified version had been watered down to a great extent, particularly with respect to the language on executive agreements. See Richard B. Bernstein and Jerome Agel, *Amending America* (New York: Random House, 1993). See also James L. Sundquist, *Constitutional Reform and Effective Government* (Washington, DC: The Brookings Institution, 1986).

11. United States House Joint Resolution 83 (1997).

12. Editorial Staff, "America First Bill," *Augusta Chronicle* (6 July 1997).

13. Ibid.

Seven

Paganism Repackaged

Bureaucrats at work on the international level have an ardent desire to eliminate any semblance of national boundaries. They seek to combine nation-states into a global federation, but of course, there are serious obstacles to achieving this objective. One such stumbling block is the marked religious distinction that forms a natural barrier between diverse groups of people. A new, generic brand of religion could prove extremely helpful in unifying the world under a single belief system, especially if such a religion appeared to seek international unity. Furthermore, since religion has traditionally separated people in accordance with their convictions, this new religious ideology would need to effectively meld the doctrines found in both eastern and western cultures. It just so happens that the religious ideas emanating from the New Age movement fulfill these requirements in a diabolically perfect manner.

Today what is termed *New Age* is actually an amalgam of many ancient concepts. Babylonian paganism and selected mythologies are combined with elements of Hinduism and Buddhism. Western pseudo-scientific language is added to form the modern day New Age philosophy. Environmentalists have found that repackaging religious ideas from the distant past can be quite useful in winning new converts.

A New Theory from Ancient Greece

James Lovelock is a British inventor and atmospheric chemist. In 1979 he unveiled a theory that ordinarily would not be advanced by someone trained in the sciences. In his premise, he synthesized and consolidated New Age beliefs that had been fomenting on the international environmental scene. William Golding, the novelist, provided Lovelock with an appropriate name for this new proposal: the "Gaia Hypothesis," named after the ancient pagan goddess of earth.[1] According to this hypothesis, the earth is not just a combination of living and non-living components, but, rather, it is a complete, living organism. Gaia theology originated in the matriarchal Minoan civilization on the isle of Crete around 2000 B.C. The Minoans worshiped the earth as a divine and powerful entity called Gaia. Other indigenous pagan cultures also viewed the earth as a sacred spirit that was to be idolized along with other gods and spirits.

When first introduced in the early 1970s, the Gaia Hypothesis attracted the most attention from theologians seeking to integrate ecology with religion, from nature lovers looking for oneness with the earth, and from activists seeking new and revolutionary ideas. As it turned out, it was a godsend, or perhaps a goddess-send, for those who wished to promote globalism, particularly environmentalists who had New Age leanings. Lovelock had basically combined biological concepts with New Age beliefs. He wrote of the qualities of life that the earth possesses, "the biosphere is a self-regulating entity with the capacity to keep our planet healthy by controlling the chemical and physical environment."[2] Astonishingly, many formerly skeptical scientists accepted his views. This is ironic since it is within scientific circles that religion is so universally shunned. Even Lovelock questioned whether the scientific community would accept something that was part religion and part philosophy, with a measure of perfunctory science thrown into the mix. Yet enthusiasm for Lovelock's theory continued to grow. In 1988 a convention aptly called Scientists on Gaia—the Symposium was held. That such a meeting of eminent physical scientists would convene to discuss a quasi-religious subject was unprecedented since the birth of modern scientific thought. It is absolutely baffling to think that a prominent group of geophysical scientists would get together to examine whether the earth could be considered a vast living system in its own right. It is even more extraordinary to realize that the entire notion was swiftly gaining momentum.[3]

New Age Infiltration

The beginning of the current infiltration of New Age into the environmental movement took place on Earth Day in 1990. This is when the concept of recognizing the earth as a living being, worthy of worship, was introduced to the world at large. Many environmental publications view biblical teachings as the cause of significant ecological problems. In an issue of *Time* magazine that was dedicated to environmental matters, the Bible, and in particular the book of Genesis, was cited as one of the reasons for man's mistreatment of nature.[4] A significant number of environmentalists dislike the Book of Genesis, especially when it comes to the part where man is given dominion over the earth and told to "be fruitful and multiply."[5] In the opinion of these zealots, the spread of Judeo-Christian beliefs led to the development of the type of technology that would eventually cause harm to the earth. It would, therefore, only be natural for individuals of this ilk to gravitate toward a belief system that viewed nature as divine.

An Earth Oriented Religion

A New Age watershed classic was born when Marilyn Ferguson wrote her book, *The Aquarian Conspiracy*,[6] a 450-page treatise that describes in detail the growing presence of the New Age philosophy. It was a bestseller in the 1980s and is still available in print and accessible at many public libraries. One of its chapters, "The Whole Earth Conspiracy," envisions a transformed society that would change the world through a revolution in consciousness.[7] In a relatively brief period of time, this vision has taken shape and become a foreboding reality in segments of our country and vast areas of our world.

The Heart of the Operation

The Episcopal Cathedral of Saint John the Divine is located in New York City's upper West Side. It is the second largest Gothic cathedral in the world and is often referred to as the "Green Cathedral." Any given New Age directory will list the Cathedral of Saint John the Divine as the center for ecological New Age ideas. The Cathedral has within it different chapels consistent in the theme that members can achieve contact with the earth goddess. It regularly holds ecological conferences that bring New Age spiritual leaders and environmental scientists together with prominent politicians.[8] The Episcopal Cathedral of Saint John the Divine houses a number of global and mystical organizations, such as the Lindisfarne Association, the Gaia Institute, and the Temple of Understanding. As it would happen, all of these ideas and entities are curiously interconnected.

Maurice Strong

At times, one can go through the cathedral and hear Maurice Strong speaking. Maurice Strong is a regent of the Cathedral of Saint John the Divine and is active in the Lindisfarne Association. Strong's organization, the Earth Council, has been working together with Mikhail Gorbachev's group, the Green Cross, busily drafting international pacts. In addition, Strong has supported many New Age movements in the United States. His diverse global activities have been orchestrated with the philosophical bent of a long time believer in the establishment of a new world religion.

Strong wields considerable influence in both the business and political worlds. His titles are numerous. He is the senior adviser to the UN secretary general and an adviser for the Rockefeller and Rothschild trusts. He is director of the International Union for the Conservation of Nature, senior adviser to the president of the World Bank, chairman of the Earth Council, chairman of the World Resources Institute, and co-chairman of the Council of the World Economic Forum. He was secretary general of the 1972 Earth Summit in Stockholm and the 1992 Earth Summit in Rio de Janeiro. Observers of the United Nations place Maurice Strong on the top of the short list to become the next secretary general of the UN. No one is better positioned or as well-connected to achieve this increasingly powerful position.[9]

The Lindisfarne Association

An additional assembly that operates out of the Cathedral of Saint John the Divine is the Lindisfarne Association. According to their literature, Lindisfarne is financed by grants from the Rockefeller Foundation and other globally inclined benefactors. Lindisfarne has constructed an auxiliary temple for cult practices in Crestone, Colorado. The building is intentionally shaped like the female form to symbolize the nourishing Mother earth goddess. The temple was located in Crestone because the Canadian billionaire, Maurice Strong, purchased approximately 160,000 acres there. New Age organizations from all over the world are brought to this enormous ranch in an attempt to establish it as a center for this form of spirituality. The inevitable goal of the association's activity is to promote nature worship as a single, global religious faith.

The National Religious Partnership for the Environment

The National Religious Partnership for the Environment (NRPE) is the establishment that was set up ostensibly to oversee in American churches the promotion of ideas such as the ones mentioned above. Concepts of nature worship, environmental Sabbaths, and ecological spirituality abound in the activities of the NRPE. Like-minded thinkers such as Al Gore, Tim Wirth, James Parks Morton, and Carl Sagan, among others, created the group at the Cathedral of Saint John the Divine. The organization has targeted every major house of worship in North America for infiltration and dissemination of propaganda. The NRPE has spent millions of dollars to advance its brand of theology in traditional religious communities. Specialized training for clergy is offered in order to accomplish the goal of changing the structure of society. Most New Age directories list the NRPE as a kindred organization. The NRPE receives funding from many sympathetic charitable foundations.

Albert Gore

The Cathedral of Saint John the Divine was also the setting for a momentous event that featured Albert Gore. For this particular occasion, Gore put on priestly vestments and preached to a congregation of humans, animals, and plants. In Al Gore's misguided book, *Earth in the Balance*,[10] he specifically cites James Lovelock's theory described earlier. In a chapter entitled "Environmentalism of the Spirit," Gore takes an "everything is everything" approach to environmental spirituality. While praising the religious tradition of pagan religions, he elevates the spirituality of nature and opens the door for a reintroduction of primitive beliefs. Gore points out that a growing number of anthropologists and archeologists hold that in prehistoric Europe and throughout much of the world, the prevailing ideology is based upon the worship of a single earth goddess who was assumed to be the fount of all life. He speaks of this sacredness of the earth while also lauding Eastern religions and the Bahai faith.[11] He credits some of the individuals who have contributed to his personal spirituality, namely, James Parks Morton, Carl Sagan, and Tim Wirth.

David Spangler

In another example of the intertwining nature of these groups, David Spangler is a faculty member at Lindisfarne and the author of *Reflections on the Christ*.[12] In his disturbing work, Spangler praises the name of Lucifer, the Evil One who is abhorred by Christians, Jews, and Moslems alike. In a twisted paraphrase of a passage from the last book of the Bible, Spangler declares that "Lucifer, like Christ, stands at the door of man's consciousness and knocks."[13] He exhorts the reader to accept Lucifer and promises that, if accepted, "Lucifer works within each of us, . . . Lucifer comes to give us the final gift of wholeness. If we accept it, then he is free and we are free."[14] Spangler refers to this as the Luciferic initiation, which is the entryway to the New Age.

James Parks Morton

Included among other members of the cathedral's entourage is James Parks Morton, who became the dean of the Cathedral of Saint John the Divine in 1972. He immediately put into motion some radical changes in Judeo-Christian constructs. Morton began to restructure the church calendar. Rather than continuing the traditional practices of penitence and suffering during the season of Lent, he wanted to focus Lenten worship in a different direction. Morton suggested, "Let's talk about the suffering of the earth, the passion of water. Let's talk about Jesus in earth—God incarnate in the flesh of earth, the flesh of water, the flesh of the elements of creation and how that creation is suffering—the passion of the creation."[15]

In 1979 Morton established the first Sun Day Celebration. He gathered speakers on environmental subjects and held an environmental fair. In that same year, James Lovelock published his book, *Gaia: A New Look at Life on Earth*.[16] Morton conveniently held a party for James Lovelock, who was then able to give the first public presentation of the Gaia Hypothesis from the pulpit of the renowned cathedral. Lovelock's Gaia Institute wound up being housed at the Cathedral of Saint John the Divine. Morton fully embraces the Gaia Hypothesis, believing that the earth is, in essence, the body of Christ. In fact, he gave a sermon that year, "Earth as God's Body," preaching a pantheistic theology about the whole of creation being the body of Christ.[17] He is intent on making the sacred earth language a part of mainstream speech.

The Temple of Understanding

The Temple of Understanding, a building constructed on a large multi-acre parcel in Washington, D.C., was a creation of the United Lodge of Theosophists of New York. It was made possible through the tax-exempt Lucis Trust and is a significant symbol of the United Nations Theosophy-based belief system. Its main headquarters are at the Cathedral of Saint John the Divine.

Marketing the New Age

It is becoming abundantly clear that New Age spirituality is really nothing new at all. It is simply a collection of some old pagan beliefs cleverly repackaged and marketed to a public thirsting for spirituality. Books on the subject of nature worship are flourishing. One title that is particularly troubling is *Celebrating the Great Mother: A Handbook of Earth-Honoring Activities for Parents and Children,* by Cait Johnson and Maura D. Shaw.[18] The book is a manual written to assist parents, caregivers, teachers, and counselors in bringing children into rituals that celebrate seasonal cycles and help to reclaim the spiritual roots of modern holidays. It shows how earth-centered activities and ceremonies can be incorporated into simple daily routines. The *Midwest Book Review* describes the book as

> a handbook of Earth-honoring activities for parents and children providing a family-oriented approach to the rituals of celebration, giving parents and adults insight into the spiritual experiences which will inspire kids and help them to understand holiday meanings.

The table of contents is a virtual idolater's delight, with chapter titles such as "Ancient Festivals: A Sense of Coming Home," "Discovering the Goddess," "Nature's Sacred World," "Dreams: Messages from Underground," "Self-empowerment in a Pouch: Making and Using Talismans," "The Magical Inner Journey," and "The Family Altar."

Part I of the *Handbook for Earth-Connected Parenting*, gives techniques for developing a child's inner wisdom through the use of dream journals, visualization, and talismans, which are astrologically related objects considered to have magical properties. Part II of the book provides details on "The Festivals," outlining ways in which parents and children can celebrate autumn and spring equinoxes, winter and summer solstices, and periods of harvest.

Even many of our leading universities have jumped on the goddess bandwagon. Courses in goddess worship are being offered through various disciplines, including education and theology. Some bookstores have entire sections devoted to books on goddess worship. The titles themselves are quite troubling. Below is a sample of readily-available titles:

Ariadne's Thread: A Workbook of Goddess Magic

Casting the Circle: A Women's Book of Ritual

Evoking the Goddess: Initiation, Worship, and the Eternal Goddess: Mother of Living Nature

The Goddess Workbook: A Guide to the Feminine Spiritual Experience

Goddesses for Every Season

The Great Cosmic Mother: Rediscovering the Religion of the Earth

Goddess: Myths of the Female Divine

Mysteries of the Dark Moon: The Healing Power of the Dark Goddess

The Spiral Dance: A Rebirth of the Ancient Religion of the Great Goddess

The ideas expressed in these books reflect a yearning to supplant currently held religious convictions with the notion of an ancient Mother goddess. The traditional understanding of God the Father is described as a detrimental, patriarchal point of view that is harming the planet. In this perspective, God becomes feminized and, therefore, in the advocates' minds, a much more compassionate figure of worship.

When scientists abandon reason and clergy discard ortho-
doxy to embrace and promote a common religious doctrine, we
can be assured that there is mischief afoot. The public is being
sold a product as something "new," complete with the appropriate and attractive, but misleading, mercantile packaging. In the
spirit of "let the buyer beware," the constituent consumer of this
brand of worship need only scrape away the thin veneer to find
something entirely different, yet strangely familiar, lurking beneath the surface. Rather than innovation in religious thought,
what is being peddled turns out to be a movement that is quite
ancient but was previously rejected by our forebears as a detriment to the pursuit of truth. As we shall discover, traditional
faith is treated contrary to this repackaged version by government
at both the national and international levels.

Notes

1. See James E. Lovelock, *Gaia* (New York: Oxford University Press,
1979).

2. Ibid., Preface.

3. Stephen Schneider, *Scientists on Gaia* (Boston: MIT Press, 1991).

4. *Time* (1 June 1992).

5. Genesis 1:28.

6. Marilyn Ferguson, *The Aquarian Conspiracy* (New York: The Putnam
Publishing Group, 1980).

7. Ibid., 405-417.

8. Literature available from the Episcopal Cathedral of Saint John the
Divine, Public Information Office, 1047 Amsterdam Ave., New York,
NY 10025.

9. See James Hirsen, "A Strong Scent of Tyranny," *Covenant Syndicate*
2, No. 75 (January 1998). http://capo.org/opeds/scentoft.htm. See also
Samantha Smith, *Goddess Earth* (Lafayette, LA: Huntington House,
1994).

10. Albert Gore, *Earth in the Balance* (New York: Houghton Mifflin,
1992).

11. Ibid., 260.

12. David Spangler, *Reflections on the Christ* (Scotland: Findhorn Foundation, 1977).

13. Constance Cumbey, *The Hidden Dangers of the Rainbow* (Lafayette, LA: Huntington House, 1983), 139.

14. Ibid.

15. Interview with the Rev. James Parks Morton conducted by Alan Atkisson. Originally published in *IN CONTEXT* No. 24 (Late Winter, 1990): 16.

16. James Lovelock, *Gaia: A New Look at Life on Earth* (Oxford: Oxford University Press: 1995).

17. Atkisson, *IN CONTEXT*, 16.

18. Cait Johnson and Maura D. Shaw, *Celebrating the Great Mother: A Handbook of Earth-Honoring Activities for Parents and Children* (Rochester, Vermont: Destiny Books, 1995).

Eight

Church and State:
Selective Separation

During the last forty years, religious expression in public life has been under assault. Those who mount the attacks constantly invoke the phrase "separation of church and state." So often we hear that the United States Constitution guarantees the separation of church and state. The notion is repeated with such frequency that most people assume these words are actually contained within the body of the Constitution. Surprisingly, the Constitution never makes the statement at all. The First Amendment merely says: "Congress shall make no law respecting an establishment of religion or prohibiting the free exercise thereof."[1] The purpose of the Establishment Clause of the First Amendment is to bar the state from establishing a religion or favoring one religious view over another.

The pronouncement of separation of church and state originated in a letter by Thomas Jefferson, written in 1802 to a group of Baptist pastors in Danbury, Connecticut. It was written to assure those Baptist pastors that Jefferson's unorthodox view of Christianity would not be forced upon the nation while he was president. The Supreme Court has used Jefferson's language to create an unfounded interpretation of the First Amendment.

Dispute Over Bus Money

The separation issue really took flight in New Jersey in 1946. The township of Ewing decided to reimburse parents for the money they spent on bus transportation to school for their children. Under the New Jersey law, parents of children who were attending parochial schools were eligible for reimbursement along with parents of public schoolchildren. A taxpayer filed a lawsuit alleging that the reimbursement for the parochial schoolchildren was unconstitutional. The case went through the usual judicial channels before eventually arriving on the doorstep of the United

States Supreme Court. A friend of the court brief in support of the taxpayer who had brought the suit was filed by the American Civil Liberties Union (ACLU). In making its decision, the Supreme Court held that the reimbursement was not in violation of the Constitution. However, this was the first time that the Court used some language that would have far-reaching and, in many cases, devastating effects upon religious expression in our country. The Court actually set a new tone for the interpretation of the First Amendment by its use of the following language: "The First Amendment has erected a wall between church and state. That wall must be kept high and impregnable."[2]

Prayer is Prohibited

The next time the United States Supreme Court had a chance to significantly speak on the subject of religious expression was in 1962. The board of education of a school district located in Hyde Park, New York, had directed the principal to require that a morning prayer be said in each class with the teacher present. If you were listening outside the door of a Hyde Park classroom in the early morning you would have heard, "Almighty God, we acknowledge our dependence upon Thee and we beg Thy blessings upon us, our parents, our teacher, and our country." The parents of ten of the students in the school district filed a lawsuit questioning the constitutionality of this morning prayer. The lower courts upheld that the prayer was constitutional as long as students were not compelled to participate. However, the U.S. Supreme Court held that the First Amendment prohibited this prayer, even if it was denominationally neutral, and even if pupils who wished to do so could remain silent or be excused from the room while the prayer was recited.[3]

Beating up on the Bible

In 1963 the U.S. Supreme Court simultaneously heard cases from Pennsylvania and Maryland dealing with school prayer. Pennsylvania had passed a law in 1959 that required ten Bible verses to be read without comment at the opening of each school day. The law provided that any child could be excused from the reading through a written request of a parent or guardian. In Maryland, the city of Baltimore had adopted a school rule that each day would begin with a reading. The rule specified that a chapter from the Bible or the Lord's Prayer would be read without comment. Students could choose not to participate if parents so requested.[4] In addressing both cases, the U.S. Supreme Court held that under the Constitution, passages from the Bible may not be read, nor can the Lord's Prayer be recited, in the public schools, even though individual students could be excluded from attending or participating upon the written request of their parents.

The Kindergarten Prayer Police

In 1962 Elihu Oshinsky, principal of Public School No. 184 in Whitestone, New York, ordered the teachers to stop allowing kindergartners to engage in the following prayer prior to eating their cookies and milk: "God is great, God is good, and we thank him for our food." Apparently Oshinsky felt this was worthy of a directive in order to protect the children from any potential harm that participation in this activity might cause. Oshinsky also instructed the teachers of the kindergarten classes to stop the students from reciting the following prayer in the afternoon session: "Thank you for the world so sweet, thank you for the food we eat, thank you for the birds that sing, thank you, God, for everything." Just to be sure that the little ones were completely safeguarded, Oshinsky ordered the teachers to cease saying any prayer in any classroom in Public School No. 184. The parents of fifteen of the twenty-one children from various religious faiths filed a lawsuit in the District Court for the Eastern District of New York. The trial court granted summary judgment to these plaintiff parents. This meant that a trial was denied on the merits, and, consequently, the children would be allowed to pray. However, the defendants decided to appeal. A friend of the court brief was filed by the New York Civil Liberties Union. The federal court held that the state does not have to permit even student-initiated prayers in public schools and directed the court to dismiss the parents' complaint, thereby reversing the summary judgment in the defendants' favor. As a result of this decision, the children would not be allowed to pray.[5] They stated, "After all that the states have been told about keeping the wall between the church and state high and impregnable, it would be rather bitter irony to chastise New York for having built the wall too tall and too strong."[6]

Non-prayer Nonsense

Parents who wanted their children to be able to have some form of religious observance in the public schools were trying to find a way to comply with previous Supreme Court decisions. In the 1965-66 school year at the Elwood Public School in DeKalb County, Illinois, a kindergarten class taught by Esther Watne prayed: "We thank you for the flowers so sweet, we thank you for the food we eat, we thank you for the birds that sing, we thank you for everything." Some parents brought a lawsuit to have the court halt this perceived threat to the kindergarten class. This was done even though no specific reference to God was expressed in this version of the classic prayer. In June of 1966 the U.S. District Court of Illinois rejected the attempt to seek an injunction against this activity, and so the children would be allowed to continue their practice of praying.[7] However, the small victory would be short-lived. The higher Federal Court of Appeals held this prayer to be an establishment of religion and, therefore, unconstitutional.[8]

The Battle of the Cross

A public park overlooks the city of Eugene, Oregon, from the crest of Skinner's Butte. The piece of land it sits on was donated to the city. From the late 1930s until 1964, a series of wooden crosses had been erected in the park. As each cross became old and deteriorated, a new cross would be put in its place. Thus, a community tradition had been established. At both Christmas and Easter, decorative lights were placed upon the crosses, and they could be seen from great distances.

On 28 November 1964, three local firms, Eugene Sand and Gravel, Inc., Hamilton Electric, and J.F. Oldham and Son, Inc., constructed a concrete cross on the crest of Skinner's Butte. The cross stood fifty-one feet high. Neon lighting was installed to light the cross before Christmas and Easter, just as the smaller crosses had been illuminated over the decades. The display prompted the usual litigation and the case moved through the Oregon civil court system to the highest court in the state. The question before the Supreme Court of Oregon was whether or not the concrete cross had to be removed because its very existence was unconstitutional. The American Civil Liberties Union of Oregon filed a friend of the court brief. The trial court had required removal of the cross and the city did not appeal, but one of the defendants, Eugene Sand and Gravel, did. The Supreme Court of Oregon held that the erection and maintenance of the cross was not a religious activity and therefore was not unconstitutional. The trial court's conclusion was reversed and the cross was allowed to stand.[9] Meanwhile, the opponents of the cross did not give up. Although the court's decisions went through a complicated seven-year string of appeals and reversals due to the perpetual legal attacks by opponents of the cross display, a charter amendment was approved by the voters of the city accepting the cross as a memorial to United States war veterans. This enabled the Supreme Court of Oregon to finally allow the cross to stand without dispute.[10]

Congressional Record Deemed Inappropriate

In New Jersey, in September 1969, the Netcong Board of Education adopted a resolution that created a class period in which students could engage in the free exercise of religion. The resolution allowed the schools to create the specified period in whatever manner and form the superintendent considered best. In the Netcong High School gymnasium, just before school began, students who wished to join in their designated class period would sit or stand in the bleachers of the gymnasium. A student volunteer would then read directly from the Congressional Record of the United States. The reading would include remarks made by the congressional chaplain along with the date, volume number, and body of those proceedings. After the reading, students would sit and reflect about what they had just heard.

In this case, the commissioner of education sued the New Jersey Board of Education to put an end to the activity. The Superior Court of New Jersey heard the case in 1970. The court held that this program was unconstitutional despite the fact that it was purely a voluntary activity and the students were reading from the Congressional Record, an official publication of the United States.[11]

Two Minutes Too Many

Efforts nevertheless continued on the part of schools and parents to have some semblance of religious expression for their children while complying with new restrictions. In Leyden,

Massachusetts, in 1969, the school committee of Leyden adopted a resolution. Once again, early in the morning before classes started, the students were permitted to engage in prayer or spiritual expression in the classroom. The average duration of the exercise was to be two to three minutes. Generally, one of the children or teachers would read from a Bible, anthology, or other inspirational text. On some occasions, traditional or innovative prayers would be said. The entire activity was completely voluntary.

The resolution was given to the teachers of the Leyden Elementary School, and they were informed that it was their choice to decide whether they wanted to participate.[12] The Supreme Court of Massachusetts heard this case and held that these activities were unconstitutional, even though students and teachers were not required to participate and there was no prescribed form for the religious activity.

The Ten Commandments Are Torn Down

In Kentucky, in 1978, the legislature passed a statute which required that a copy of the Ten Commandments be posted on the wall of each public classroom in the state. In 1980 the Kentucky Supreme Court ruled that posting a copy of the Ten Commandments on the wall was unconstitutional.[13] The wall of separation was growing higher, thicker, and a whole lot stronger. Earlier the same year, with almost identical facts, the North Dakota District Court came to the exact same holding, ruling that a North Dakota law which required the display of the Ten Commandments in every classroom violated the Establishment Clause of the First Amendment and was unconstitutional.[14]

Student Choice Denied

During the 1977-79 school years at Chandler High School in Chandler, Arizona, school assemblies were held. The Chandler Student Council had requested permission to open their assemblies with prayer, so a student was selected to lead the devotion. The student was free to choose the manner and words in which the prayer was delivered. In 1981 the United States Court of Appeals for the Ninth Circuit ruled on the question of whether or not this activity was constitutional. The court held that even though it was at the student council's request and students could choose whatever form of prayer they desired, the Establishment Clause of the First Amendment was violated. The issue of whether or not participation in the school assemblies was voluntary did not matter.[15]

No Release for Religious Classes

In 1981 the United States Court of Appeals of the Tenth Circuit dealt with a Utah State Board of Education program supervised by the city of Logan, Utah. The Utah program involved the release of students during the school day to take elective religious courses. The public schools were involved in gathering attendance slips that had been prepared and provided by the schools, and students who took these religious programs were granted elective credit. Based on these particulars, the program was held to have violated the Establishment Clause of the First Amendment.[16]

Benediction Cancelled

For at least twenty years prior to May 1985, the Decatur High School graduation ceremonies opened with a prayer. In 1994 the Iowa Civil Liberties Union wrote to the school board in Decatur County, Iowa, and demanded that they abandon their tradition of a prayer at the graduation ceremony. When a civil action was subsequently brought, the United States District Court held in May 1985 that a religious invocation and benediction at a graduation ceremony violated the Establishment Clause of the First Amendment.[17]

In 1985 and again in 1986 the Court of Appeals of Oregon decided that a religious invocation at a high school commencement violated the Constitution.[18]

Silence is Muzzled

In June 1985 the U.S. Supreme Court dealt with the constitutionality of a 1981 Alabama statute that authorized a one minute period of silence in all public schools "for meditation or voluntary prayer."[19] The Court held that this law violated the First Amendment and therefore was unconstitutional.[20]

Eviction of Nativity Scene

For decades, holiday displays created a festive spirit and livened up the atmosphere in downtown Pittsburgh. Since 1981, during the Christmas season a Christian nativity scene was placed at the staircase of the Allegheny County Courthouse, a prominent building in downtown Pittsburgh. It was donated by a Roman Catholic group, the Holy Name Society, and bore a sign to that effect. Another display was an eighteen-foot Chanukah menorah, which was placed just outside the city-county building next to the city's forty-five foot decorated Christmas tree. The menorah was owned by a Jewish group, Chabad. Along with some local residents, the American Civil Liberties Union filed suit in December of 1986 to have the court end both displays on the grounds that they violated the Establishment Clause of the First Amendment of the Constitution. The trial court denied the request of the plaintiffs and the displays were allowed to remain. The plaintiffs appealed, though, and the court of appeals ruled in their favor, ordering the displays to be removed.[21] The case went all the way to the U.S. Supreme Court. The High Court ruled that the nativity scene violated the Constitution, but the menorah display did not because it was deemed to be more like a Christmas tree.[22]

These are some of the major landmark cases in the legal area. Scores of other examples could be provided to demonstrate the incremental loss of religious freedom that is occurring over time. Rulings have been expanded in recent years by local courts, policies, and legislation resulting in a public square that is increasingly secularized and sanitized of all religious references. Nonetheless, the continual erosion of traditional religious expression stands in marked contrast to the preferred status given to "acceptable" religious beliefs and practices of UN organizations.

Church and State Intermingle at the Global Level

It is disturbing to see the distorted manner in which the Establishment Clause of the Constitution is used to undermine public religious life. It is equally troublesome to see the amazing way that politically correct notions of religion are promoted at the international level. Exactly who is providing the financial backing to promote such ideas? It is the American citizenry, unwittingly subsidizing this ideology with their hard earned tax dollars.

Deep within the confines of the New York City headquarters of the United Nations is a room that is conspicuous in its inappropriateness. It is particularly curious that this room is found in a government-financed body that promulgates international law. Located in the northwest end of the entrance level of the General Assembly building is what is known as the UN Meditation Room. In this eerie, dimly lit room, there is a large block in the center that appears to be an altar. Various kinds of religious ceremonies are performed here on a regular basis. The designated hours of operation are restricted, and the area is only available for use from 8 A.M. to 9 A.M. and from 11 A.M. to 2 P.M. Tourists who come to the United Nations building will find that the Meditation Room is not open to the public, nor are there any scheduled tours of this space.

In a book called *Spiritual Politics: Changing the World from the Inside Out,* Corinne McLaughlin and Gordon Davidson wrote about the activities that take place in the UN Meditation Room. They describe the room as useful in providing mystical experiences to United Nations officials. McLaughlin and Davidson speak about "vast beings" with whom UN officials come in contact while inside what they describe as the "holiest of holies on the planet," the UN Meditation Room.[23] American taxpayers are essentially providing hundreds of millions of dollars for what are, in reality, religious programs. For example, the environmental Sabbath that was mentioned earlier is, in fact, an official United Nations proposal. It basically advances the idea that a day of the week should be set aside to honor the earth. This promotion is under the auspices of the United Nations Environmental Program.

Additionally, McLaughlin and Davidson have long been involved with the Temple of Understanding. The Temple has been associated with United Nations activities for a long time. The Temple has plans to construct a Peace Pyramid in Washington, D.C. It will be a structure dedicated to worship of the earth, complete with a large hologram for worshipers to present offerings and adoration. The list of spiritual advisers and assorted gurus that have been a part of the United Nations New Age worship programs is considerably long. Many are particularly noteworthy and warrant our attention and examination.

Jean Houston, Spiritual Mentor

Jean Houston, who has had significant involvement with the
United Nations herself, is a spiritual adviser to Hillary Rodham
Clinton.[24] Houston has chaired the United Nations Conference
on World Religion. She also works closely with UNICEF and is
involved with other international religious activities. Houston is
described as one who believes in spirits and historical connections
to the past and other worlds. She was the one who led Mrs.
Clinton through the famed conversations with Eleanor Roosevelt
and Mahatma Gandhi. She has a reputation for placing people
into trances and conducting experiments with psychedelic drugs.
Houston is said to have also influenced Mrs. Clinton's decision
to go to China and speak at the UN International Women's
Conference.[25]

Robert Muller

Robert Muller has been involved with the United Nations
for thirty-three years and has served in numerous capacities, including assistant secretary general. He wrote a book, *New Genesis: Shaping a Global Spirituality.* In this work, he stated that the
world religions have an obligation to foster global spirituality. He
believes that in order for humanity to survive this threatening
period of global existence, we must engage in a unified global
response.[26]

Muller's perspective on the religiosity of the United Nations
can be likened to the Moslem devotion to Mecca or the Catholic
reverence for the Vatican. He described the headquarters of the
United Nations as a source of revelation when he wrote:

> The tall Secretariat building of the UN is an edifice of human
> hope and dream jutting into the universe and receiving from
> that universe increasingly clearer messages. Perhaps the time
> has come when we will understand the full significance of our
> cosmic evolution.[27]

In the chapter "Prayer and Meditation at the United Nations," Muller spoke of the creation of a new global scripture
when he said:

> Little by little, a planetary prayer book is thus being com-
> posed by an increasingly united humanity seeking its one-
> ness, its happiness, its consciousness, its peace, its justice and

its full participation in the continuing process of creation and miracle of life. Once again, but this time on a universal scale, humankind is seeking no less than its reunion with the divine, its transcendence into ever higher forms of life. Hindus call our earth Brahma, or God, for they rightly see no difference between our earth and the divine. This ancient simple truth is slowly dawning again upon humanity.[28]

This reference to earth and the divine as synonymous is just another way of describing the worship of the earth as pursued by environmental followers of Gaia. Those who follow Judeo-Christian traditions may not be aware of these significant developments. It is important that the information is made available so that those who care about the issue of religious freedom are prepared to respond.

Crisis Mentality

Since the United Nations has adopted the role of promoter of religion, it is worthwhile to reexamine the UN statement on religious freedom contained in the Covenant on Civil and Political Rights: "Freedom to manifest one's religion or belief may be subject only to such limitations as are prescribed by law and are necessary to protect public safety, order, health, or morals or the fundamental rights and freedoms of others."[29] This language contains an ominous loophole. The state may take away the fundamental freedom to worship with a simple rationalization. As long as the deprivation of religious liberty is necessary to protect, for example, the public order, it may be accomplished with impunity.

Under the paradigm espoused by the UN and expressed in the Gaia Hypothesis, the only hope for the survival of humankind is to worship and accommodate nature. If we do so, we will become God. If we fail to respond, we will be destroyed by nature in an almost punitive manner. The horror and fear of such punishment through natural disasters is reflected in the crisis mentality used to promote environmental initiatives. It is this appeal to fear that we hear more and more frequently. We are given stern warnings that we must act now before it's is too late concerning things like global warming and population growth.

For example, the Sierra Club book *Well Body, Well Earth* cautions that because most of us choose to live in the urban or

suburban setting without much contact with the earth, "we require something like visualization to help us get in touch with
our planet."[30] Readers are instructed that "in all the visualization
exercises that follow, the goal is to guide your awareness so that
you can benefit from the living Earth by taking an active role as
a homeostatic agent of the noosphere."[31]

The book speaks of the priestesses of Gaia, who were trained
in the art of visualization and dedicated their lives to studying the
spirit of the living earth. These priestesses would consult with
Gaia to solve problems, such as where to plant their fields or how
to deal with childbirth. The book also provides some history for
validation, stating that "in Greece, for example, when people
wanted help in solving difficult problems, they consulted the
Oracle at Delphi. Incidentally, the priests acknowledged a spirit
of the living Earth, for which the Greek name was Gaea [sic]."[32]
This modern day nature worship is nothing new. It is identical
to ancient pagan practices that existed and were spoken about in
the Bible. As we shall see in future chapters, a nature religion
mentality helps to create the consciousness necessary to attack
individual rights, particularly those concerning private property.

Theosophy

Theosophy has been described as an archaic wisdom religion
that was once known in every ancient country having claims to
civilization. It is an early mix of eastern and western belief systems that forms the bedrock for the modern New Age movement. Theosophy was established in 1875 by Madame Helena
Petrovna Blavatsky and Colonel Henry Steel Olcott. Blavatsky
spoke of an ancient fraternity of adepts that provided a source of
secret knowledge. She claimed to be their agent-messenger to
bring this wisdom to the world.[33] One of Blavatsky's books, *The
Secret Doctrine*,[34] is a foundational sourcebook for New Age belief
systems. Blavatsky's teachings actually foreshadowed Lovelock's
Gaia Hypothesis by characterizing the earth as a living organism.[35]

Blavatsky gave great praise to the ancient pagan beliefs. She
dismissed belief in the Bible as a blasphemy against a deity she
referred to as the "divine majesty." According to Blavatsky, Lucifer was to be held in greater esteem than Jehovah, much in the
same way eco-New Agers like David Spangler hold Lucifer in

high regard. In 1887 Blavatsky even created a magazine that she named *Lucifer.*[36]

Blavatsky's desire to elevate the devil is illustrated in a small sampling of her statements. "Lucifer is a divine and terrestrial light, 'the Holy Ghost' and 'Satan,' at one and the same time."[37] Blavatsky equated Satan and God by referring to them as brothers. "Satan was a Son, and an angel of God. With all the Semitic nations, the Spirit of the Earth was as much the Creator in his own realm as the Spirit of the Heavens. They were twin brothers and interchangeable in their functions, when not two in one."[38] Not content with merely making God Satan's twin, Blavatsky also made God the first murderer. "The great Serpent of the Garden of Eden and the 'Lord God' are identical, and so are Jehovah and Cain."[39] Undoubtedly, Blavatsky has an entirely different interpretation of the traditional religious concept known as the fall of man. She declared, "The Fall was the result of man's knowledge, for his 'eyes were opened.' Indeed, he was taught Wisdom and the hidden knowledge by the 'Fallen Angel.' "[40] Blavatsky's view of creation reflected her polytheism. "Man is, beyond any doubt, formed physically out of the dust of the Earth, but his creators and fashioners were many."[41]

At the beginning of the twentieth century, the Theosophical Society was taken over by Annie Besant and Alice Bailey. The original publishing company of the Theosophical Society was called the Lucifer Trust Publishing Company. Of course, with a name like that, it received a less than favorable reception from Christian America, so Bailey renamed it Lucis Trust. It is still publishing works today and is intimately involved with United Nations activities.

Early theosophical writings reflect the foundational beliefs of nature worship and describe how man's presence and the advances in technology have disrupted the order of nature. All of the beliefs provide strong rationales for the environmental movement's extreme notion that in order to save the earth, drastic changes to our economy, social structure, and culture must be dictated. All through the theosophical writings, references to the process of implementing what New Agers call "The Plan" can be found. The Plan, which has actually been in existence since ancient times, ostensibly came from a mysterious Tibetan master who telepathically communicated the knowledge to Blavatsky.[42]

At the opening prayer of the Earth Summit and in ceremonies that have taken place in the UN Meditation Room, the Great Invocation of Theosophy has been used. It closes with these words: "From this centre which we call the race of men, let the Plan of Love and Light work out. And may it seal the door where evil dwells. Let Light and Love and Power restore the Plan on Earth."[43]

It is believed that there is a psychic power generated by humanity and it will unite the world. This psychic force will usher in the universal religion and give birth to a new kingdom in nature. This is the reason that the Great Invocation was used at the Earth Summit and is prayed in the Meditation Room of the United Nations. It is Alice Bailey's belief that the Great Invocation will cause Father Sun and Mother Earth to mate. Bailey states in one of her many works, *The Rays and the Initiations: A Treatise on the Seven Rays*,[44] that there is a planetary triad composed of Earth (Gaia), Venus (Lucifer), and the Sun (Shumbala), and that the numerology for this nature base triad is the number 666.[45] Bailey also states that those who will be initiated into this New Age religion will receive what will be termed "the mark of a savior," and it will be an indication of a new kind of salvation.[46]

Consistent with the above belief, this new salvation will be where man becomes God and, at the same time, is unified with the natural world. The Plan indicates a disregard for the notion of national sovereignty. It contemplates a ruling, global body that it calls an "Economic League of Nations," which sounds very much like the United Nations. It speaks of creating one world and one humanity, a world where there would be peace.[47] In order to carry out The Plan, seed groups are to be established to expedite various specialty functions. These groups have been instituted in great numbers since the establishment of the Theosophical Society. Peace groups, environmental groups, and those that are now New Age groups have sprung from the organizations originally founded by Alice Bailey through the Lucis Trust. One of these groups, World Goodwill, was headquartered in the United Nations building in New York City until 1990. The purpose of World Goodwill was to work toward the implementation of The Plan. It is a non-governmental organization that consults with the United Nations. Other seed organizations include Planetary Citizens (created by United Nations Assistant Secretary General Robert Muller), Peace Net, and Eco Net (created through the Institute of Global Communications). The stark contrast in the manner in which taxpayer funds are used to promote religious activities at the international level when compared with the dramatic secularization of tax-funded institutions domestically is truly staggering. Perhaps even more disturbing is the preference by UN-related groups and individuals for one type of religious philosophy over all others. The practices and teachings of religious leaders of the UN speak of inclusion. Yet the cold reality is that traditional religious beliefs are not welcome in the world of global bureaucrats.

Notes

1. United States Constitution, Bill of Rights, First Amendment.

2. *Everson v. Board of Education of the Township of Ewing*, et al., 330 U.S. 1, 18 (1947).

3. *Engel v. Vitale*, 370 U.S. 422-436 (1962).

4. *Abington v. Schempp*, 374 U.S. 203, Pennsylvania Statute, p. 205; Maryland Statute, p. 211.

5. *Stein v. Oshinsky*, 348 F.2d 999 (1965).

6. Ibid., 1002.

7. *DeSpain v. DeKalb County Community School District*, 428; 255 F. Supp. 655 (1966).

8. *DeSpain v. DeKalb County Community School District*, 384; F.2nd 836 (1967).

9. *Lowe v. City of Eugene*, 451 P.2d 117 (1969).

10. *Eugene Sand and Gravel, Inc. v. City of Eugene*, OR; 558 P.2d 338 (1976).

11. *State Board of Education v. Board of Education of Netcong*, 262 A.2nd 21 (1970).

12. *Commissioner of Education v. School Community of Leyden*, 267 N. E. 2d 226, 227 (1971).

13. *Stone v. Graham*, 449 U.S. 39 (1980).

14. *Ring v. Grand Forks Public School District No. 1*, 483 F.Supp. 272 (1980).

15. *Collins v. Chandler Unified School District*, 644 F.2d 759 (1981).

16. *Lanner v. Wimmer*, 662 F.2d 1349 (1981).

17. *Graham v. Central Community School District of Decatur County*, 608 F.Supp. 531 (D.C. Iowa 1985).

18. *Kay v. Douglas School District No. 40*, 719 P.2d 875 (Or. App. 1986).

19. *Wallace v. Jaffree*, 472 U.S. 38 (1985).

20. Ibid., 48-61.

21. 842 F 2d 655 (1988).

22. *Allegheny County v. ACLU*, 492 U.S. 573 (1989).

23. Corinne McLaughlin and Gordon Davidson, *Spiritual Politics: Changing the World from the Inside Out* (New York: Ballantine Books, 1994), 318.

24. "First Lady Gets into Spirit of a New Age," *The Detroit News* (24 June 1996).

25. Bob Woodward, *The Choice* (New York: Simon & Schuster, 1996).

26. Robert Muller, *New Genesis: Shaping a Global Spirituality* (Garden City, NY: Image Books, 1984).

27. Ibid., 48-49.

28. Ibid., 49.

29. International Covenant on Civil and Political Rights, Article 18 (3).

30. Mike Samuels and Hal Zina Bennett, *Well Body, Well Earth: The Sierra Club Environmental Sourcebook* (San Francisco: Sierra Club Books, 1983), 68.

31. Ibid.

32. Ibid.

33. Theosophy Library Online. http://theosophy.org/tlodocs/ blavatskybiography.htm.

34. Helena Petrovna Blavatsky, *The Secret Doctrine*, Multi-volume set, (Wheaton, IL: Quest Books, 1993).

35. Blavatsky, *The Secret Doctrine*, vol. 1, 412.

36. Theosophy Library Online. http://theosophy.org/tlodocs/ blavatskybiography.htm.

37. Blavatsky, *The Secret Doctrine*, vol. 2, 513.

38. Ibid., 477.

39. Blavatsky, *The Secret Doctrine*, vol. 1, 412.

40. Blavatsky, *The Secret Doctrine*, vol. 2, 513.

41. Blavatsky, *The Secret Doctrine*, vol. 1, 226.

42. University of the Seven Rays web site. http://www.sevenray.com/ aabinfo.htm.

43. Lucis Trust web site. http//www.lucistrust.org/gipamph.htm. See also Alice Bailey, *The Externalization of the Hierarchy* (New York: Lucis Trust, 1957).

44. Alice Bailey, *The Rays and the Initiations: A Treatise on the Seven Rays*, Vol. 5, (New York: Lucis Trust, 1970).

45. Ibid., 77-79. (The number 666 is widely used as a sacred set of numerals by the New Age movement. See Constance Cumbey, *The Hidden Dangers of the Rainbow* (Lafayette, LA: Huntington House, 1983), 22.)

46. Bailey, *The Externalization of the Hierarchy*, 191.

47. Ibid., 638-639.

Nine

Enemies of the Earth

Certain participants in the environmental movement criticize Christianity as being the most anthropocentric, or man-centered, religion in the world. In analyzing and evaluating different philosophies, environmentalists of this mentality frown upon a human oriented attitude. Instead, they favor ancient paganism and eastern religions that, in their minds, do not attempt to place man above nature. They fault Christianity for abandoning such pagan beliefs as animism and pantheism. Pantheism is the view that everything is a part of God and God is a part of everything. In other words, there is no separate and distinct Creator-God who made all of creation. Animism looks at the world and sees all living and non-living things as having a spirit or a central soul. Frequently, polytheism, or the belief in multiple deities, is an integral aspect of paganism.

Holding on to beliefs such as these, environmental extremists seek to win the hearts and minds of people by gradually changing their religious ideology. In any fight, a clear vision of the enemy tends to strengthen a movement, and battle plans are solidified when a target is distinctly identified. So it is with these environmentalists. Christian beliefs have become the enemy. Merely destroying beliefs would be insufficient. If the movement is to be truly successful, doctrines must be replaced.

Sadly, this scenario has already played out in some segments of our society. The efforts of militant environmentalists have been remarkably successful. Encouraged by their own accomplishments, they forge ahead.

Science Goes Awry

This supposed new theology has had many detrimental consequences, but one that stands out is the dangerous influence it has had on mainstream environmental scientists who end up adopting these proposals. Many of these professionals have actu-

92

ally rejected the traditional scientific principle of reason. They have accepted the premise that only a mystical communion with nature can provide true scientific understanding. In several eastern philosophies, the material world is called *maya*. It is deemed to be an illusion, with reality occurring only on a mystical or metaphysical level. This is expressed in the Shamanic beliefs set forth in the books of Carlos Castaneda and Joseph Chilton Pierce, where consensus beliefs in and of themselves constitute reality.[1]

For those who have taken on a pantheistic view of nature as somehow divine in character, scientific notions become affected. After all, how can mere science gather measurements or make predictions about a nature that is divine? Furthermore, if nature is sacred, technology becomes a violation of nature's sanctity. With this ideology in place, it follows that a human life has no greater value than that of an amoeba or, for that matter, any other life form. This concept is known as *biocentrism*. The belief that primitive man was, in fact, morally superior to modern man comes from this concept of biocentrism because, as the thinking goes, primitive man would have lived in harmony with nature and would not have attempted to subjugate other forms of life.

Ecumenical World Order

The idea of changing the fundamental belief systems of religions has been brought up at a variety of United Nations conferences. According to a prominent UN report released in 1995, elite internationalists who support and control the United Nations view religion as just another part of the social functions that must be controlled.[2]

At a UN briefing of non-governmental organizations in 1994, Samuel R. Insanally, past president of the General Assembly, mused:

> Although I am not a "religious" person . . . I do believe that the construction of a new world order requires a sense of moral obligation on the part of all nations, both developed and developing, which will give flesh to the concept of interdependence. We need in effect a spiritual catalyst to bring about change.[3]

Juan Somavia, Chile's permanent representative to the UN, has called for the presence of consciousness as an important ingredient in the UN's global efforts.[4] In 1991, at a UNESCO

Conference held in Paris, Hans Küng and Leonard Swindler proposed a document for the United Nations that would lead to a consensus on global ethics. Hans Küng had already written a book on this topic, *Global Responsibility: In Search of a New World Ethic.*[5]

In this book, Küng set forth the same pantheistic and earth-worshiping ideas that UN-supported religious groups seem to cherish. He discussed the notion that people must place a limit on their freedom now for the sake of survival of the future. Küng felt that in order to preserve the biosphere, we must have an undivided world, one where all people have the same goals and visions and, as he asserted, the same religious faith. He used the term *ecumenical world order* to describe this plan.[6] We also see the terminology *sustainable development* used in an assortment of UN documents. According to many at the United Nations, Christianity is not considered a faith that can be reconciled with sustainability. A new faith must be engineered, one that, when followed, would preserve the earth.

In 1993 the Parliament of the World's Religions met in Chicago. Those present wanted to produce a world consensus on religious concepts and ethics. At the conclusion of the conference, participants produced a document signed by most of the attendees. The formal statement that arose from the conference was called *A Global Ethic: The Declaration of the Parliament of Word's Religions.*[7] Standard religious terms are nowhere to be found in the report. It contains language that minimizes individual rights, particularly property rights. It stresses open-mindedness and implies that traditional religious views are inherently intolerant. This is not surprising considering that the conference was greatly influenced by a large number of non-traditional attendees such as the Theosophical Society of California, the Theosophical Society of America, the Temple of Understanding, Sri Chinmoy (resident guru at the UN) Center, Eckankar, the Self-Realization Fellowship, and the North American Coalition on Religion and Ecology.[8] Coincidentally, these groups also happen to be closely aligned with the United Nations.

Interference with Faith

Many documents from the United Nations are crafted to

interfere with religious liberty at will. This is consistent with the UN view of religious liberty, which is diametrically opposed to the one embodied in the founding instruments of the United States. We get a glimpse of the sort of hypocritical, discriminatory application of the law characteristic of the UN when we observe the manner in which pro-life protesters are presently treated in our country. Under the Freedom of Access to Clinic Entrances (FACE) law, first time offenders can receive a sentence of up to one year in prison and a fine of up to $100,000. Subsequent violations can result in fines as high as $250,000, or up to three years in prison for obstructing access to abortion clinics.[9] If one person is holding a peaceful, nonviolent demonstration outside a military facility, and a second person is doing the same outside an abortion clinic, under this law only the pro-life protester would be subject to federal prosecution.

Pro-life activists were recently sued by feminist organizations under federal racketeering laws. A jury verdict was rendered against the pro-life organizations. Although the judgment is in the process of being appealed, this does not negate the fact that basic injustices are occurring against select groups and individuals in society. Unfortunately, singling out one group for special legal treatment because of the content of their beliefs appears to be increasingly acceptable, particularly at the international level.

The Environment Reigns Supreme

Environmentalists claim that the ultimate goal is to preserve and protect nature for the good of all mankind. In actuality, however, the danger to mankind is from environmentalism in its excessive form. Expressing a profound hatred for all that is human, radical environmentalism seeks a natural world in which birds and trees happily exist with their needs fulfilled because human activities have been vanquished.

Protection of the environment is being advanced at every turn, from corporate boardrooms to Saturday morning cartoon shows. All Americans would agree that clean air and pure water are highly desirable conditions for which to strive in our society. However, extreme environmentalists seek to reverse the progress of technology itself. Some of their statements are particularly indicative of an underlying loathing of human activity. Philosopher Paul Taylor in *Respect for Nature: A Theory of Environmental Ethics* wrote, "The ending of the human epoch on Earth, would most likely be greeted with a hearty 'Good riddance!' "[10]

In a glowing review of Bill McKibben's *The End of Nature*,[11] biologist David M. Graber stated, "Human happiness [is] not as important as a wild and healthy planet. . . . Until such time as Homo sapiens should decide to rejoin nature, some of us can only hope for the right virus to come along."[12] Maurice Strong, the secretary general of the Earth Summit, echoed these sentiments when he outlined a portion of a proposed book that he wished to write. In an interview conducted in Canada in 1990, Strong said,

> What if a small group of world leaders were to conclude that the principal risk to the earth comes from the actions of the rich countries? And if the world is to survive, those rich countries would have to sign an agreement reducing their impact on the environment. Will they do it? . . . The group's conclusion is "no." The rich countries won't do it. They won't change. So, in order to save the planet, the group decides, isn't the only hope for the planet that the industrialized civilizations collapse? Isn't our responsibility to bring that about?[13]

Such is the sum and substance of radical environmentalism. It grieves the loss of an owl or weed, but sanctions the death of innocent humans. A more insidious, misanthropic position is difficult to imagine.

Deep Ecology

Anti-human beliefs reach their pinnacle in an environmental philosophy known as deep ecology. Deep ecologists look at the sacred earth as having a kind of infection: humankind. In this perspective, man has breached his contract with earth and become a plague upon it. Deep ecologists promote a drastic reduction in the human population and indicate that it would be a good thing for the earth if all of mankind were eliminated. In fact, it would be most desirable if technology were completely abandoned, particularly in industrialized nations, and society reverted to a non-technological status of a century or more ago. Deep ecologists take a sweeping view when considering which individuals or groups to designate as enemies of the earth. The description of an enemy becomes quite simple. It includes every-body. This reaction is based upon an intense objection to an anthropocentric view of the world. Deep ecologists hail Darwin-ian evolution as the first step in undercutting anthropocentrism.

Evolutionary theory declares that the existence of life is an accident arising from a three-and-one-half-billion-year process in which humans only played bit parts. Therefore, there is no basis for seeing human beings as more advanced than any other species. With this line of reasoning, it only follows that deep ecologists would discard the notion that mankind should be in any privileged position relative to other life forms.

The ideas of deep ecology have attracted a large following of activists among militant environmental groups. These groups are made up of people who view modern technological society as cut off from the natural world. They believe that our current society is alien and arrogant and, consequently, present day existence must be invalid. In their view, industrialized society is the result of a long line of environmentally destructive cultures that has blighted the earth since the rise of civilization. The more radi-cally-minded believers have created a new kind of criminal activ-ity. Of all the organizations who promote the use of unlawful tactics to save the environment, most familiar to the general public is the group Earth First. This organization went so far as to coin a new word for their approach. They call their methods *ecotage*, derived from the word sabotage. In their practices, they engage in subversive, and many times destructive, maneuvers in order to rescue the earth from injury. They consider ecotage as justifiable sabotage because the defense of nature must take pri-ority. Property is often damaged or destroyed in order to prevent ecological harm. Bulldozers have been burned or otherwise se-verely damaged. Major timber companies have suffered tens of millions of dollars in damage to lumber equipment and road building machinery. Their brand of environmental terrorism also includes placing spikes in trees to hinder logging, slashing tires on vehicles, or most severe, planting explosive devices, all in the name of saving the earth.[14]

Portent of Intrusion

Environmental extremists envision a primitive, fantasy world without human interference, a world where nature is worshiped for its intrinsic worth. Man is the cause of all of earth's sickness. Humanity is the intruder, the plunderer, the alien in the natural order. So, what is the problem if societies adhere to belief systems such as these? In the realm of international law, adoption of this point of view results in the regulation of any aspect of human activity that could possibly impact this perceived divine nature.

Those in positions of authority have often stirred up segments of humanity by focusing attention on a featured enemy. If an enemy is truly an obstacle that needs to be removed, the strategy of evoking emotions produces an additional advantage for those utilizing this technique. Clearly, people of traditional faith are an impediment to excessive environmentalists and their institutional allies in attaining their goals. Yet even those who are not expressly targeted by these groups should not take comfort, for as we have discovered, these fervent devotees of the environmental movement truly believe that the ultimate enemy of the earth is humanity itself.

Notes

1. See Carlos Castaneda, *The Teachings of Don Juan: A Yaqui Way of Knowledge* (New York: Simon & Schuster, 1973); Joseph Chilton Pierce, *The Crack in the Cosmic Egg: Challenging Constructs of Mind and Reality* (New York: Julian Press, 1971).

2. The Commission on Global Governance, *Our Global Neighborhood: The Report of the Commission on Global Governance* (New York: Oxford University Press, 1995), 9-10.

3. "The UN and the Spiritual Dimension," *World Goodwill Newsletter*, No. 2 (1995).

4. Ibid.

5. Hans Küng, *Global Responsibility: In Search of a New Global Ethic* (New York: Crossroad Publishing Company, 1991).

6. Ibid., p 69. See also William Norman Grigg, *Freedom on the Altar* (Appleton, WI: American Opinion Publishing, Inc., 1995).

7. Hans Küng and Karl Joseph Kuschel, *A Global Ethic: The Declaration of the Parliament of World's Religions* (New York: Continuum, 1993).

8. DePaul University, Archives and Special Collections Page. http://www.lib.depaul.edu/specccoll/.

9. Freedom of Access to Clinic Entrances Act of 1994, Title 18 U.S. Code. Signed by President Clinton in May 1994 as Senate Bill No. 636. Posted on the web at http://www.prochoice.org/violence/facetext.htm.

10. Paul Taylor, *Respect for Nature: A Theory of Environmental Ethics* (Princeton, NJ: Princeton University Press, 1986).

11. Bill McKibben, *The End of Nature* (New York: Random House, 1989).

12. David M. Graber, *Los Angeles Times,* Book Review (29 October 1989).

13. "The Wizard of Baca Grande," *West Magazine* (May 1990).

14. Dave Foreman, *Confessions of an Eco-Warrior,* audio recording (Niwot, CO: Audio Press, Inc., 1992). See also Peter C. List, *Radical Environmentalism: Philosophy and Tactics* (Belmont, CA: Wadsworth Publishing Company, 1993); Bron Raymond Taylor, *Ecological Resistance Movements: The Global Emergence of Radical and Popular Environmentalism* (New York: State University of New York Press, 1995).

Ten

The Great
Environmental Pretext

The quest to keep our water pure, our air clean, and our natural surroundings pristine remains a noble aspiration for all of us who love this majestic country and who take the notion of stewardship seriously. Yet it is becoming more and more apparent that the American way of life is gravely threatened by an excessive accumulation of governmental regulations, with very little scientific foundation or objectivity used as the basis for the creation of law.

The Messy Business of Cleanup

In 1980 Congress passed the Comprehensive Environmental Response, Compensation, and Liability Act (CERCLA) commonly known as Superfund.[1] The statute is well stocked with regulations, but short on common sense, as is typical of political attempts to regulate the environment. The legislation was meant to encourage the cleanup of environmentally contaminated sites, no doubt a worthy goal. The reasoning was that the Environmental Protection Agency would be able to sue the parties responsible for the contamination to recover the costs of remediation.

However, things did not work out quite the way they were intended. Apparently, when a site is contaminated, it can take up to a decade of testing, evaluation, and diagnosis before correction of the problem even begins. Consequently, less than fifteen percent of the contaminated sites in the country have actually been cleaned up. Ten thousand sites are pending review. It is costing over ten billion dollars each year for these activities, and it is projected that the costs could double by the year 2000.[2] Meanwhile, in attempting to address environmental problems, well-meaning legislators have caused industries to reduce the scope of their production and, in some cases, have literally forced American businesses to close. As a result, jobs have been lost. More-

100

over, because regulations create liabilities and risks that are difficult for companies to assess, numerous manufacturing plants have been given additional incentives to move out of the country. In 1989 an organization called the National Resources Defense Council alarmed Americans with the information that apples posed a threat to children because of a substance called *alar*. With Meryl Streep as their spokesperson, they managed to severely impact American apple growers for a supposed crisis that turned out to be totally unsubstantiated. Years prior to attacking the apple growing industry, this same group aggressively lobbied Congress to clean up tainted areas labeled as Superfund sites and bring them to toxic-free status. Even though this was not possible, Congress added more and more environmental statutes and regulatory requirements to an already overburdened nation.

If environmental laws make the proper disposal of toxic chemicals a legally risky endeavor, it just goes to follow that businesses are going to be dissuaded from taking part. Businesses that contemplate recycling of toxic material (and according to the CERCLA definition, "toxic material" includes almost everything) are going to be discouraged from participation in otherwise meritorious programs.

The Evolution of Environmentalism

Slowly but steadily, an enormous government bureaucracy with heavy regulatory compliance costs has been created in response to the ever-increasing demands of the environmental movement. During the 1960s and 1970s, the causes of environmental problems were more readily observed. Smoke spewing from smokestacks, odors emanating from municipal sewers, and putrid open-air dumps could easily be spotted. Solutions often involved the use of simple technology or even the banning of the egregious activity. Many times, dramatic results were produced fairly quickly. Although the benefits were highly visible, the costs tended to be concealed. They were buried in higher consumer prices and increased unemployment. The inherent strength of the American economy helped to mitigate some of the negative aspects associated with the protection of the environment.

By the 1980s, environmentalism became downright faddish. Major corporations began to advertise using environmental themes. Movie actors and actresses became spokespersons for various environmental causes. However, more subtle environmental hazards were beginning to emerge. As the public became better informed about the effect of environmental policy on employment, the cost of goods, and even tax rates, the environmental movement became more strident. Scientific realities began to be ignored, and there was a greater focus placed upon public relations. Aggressive propaganda and lobbying efforts resulted in layer upon layer of laws and regulations being enacted on the basis of exaggerated environmental claims.

Ironically, scientific facts have not stopped the Environmental Protection Agency (EPA) from asserting newer and stricter regulations. For example, in the spring of 1997 the EPA proposed new air quality standards. The administrator of the EPA, Carol Browner, told Americans that these new standards would only affect large industrial polluters. What she failed to tell the American people, though, is that any additional costs to these large industries would be passed on to American citizens in the form of higher utility bills, higher transportation costs, and higher prices for consumer goods. The Reason Foundation, a libertarian think tank based in Los Angeles, predicted that these changes alone would cost American consumers up to $120 billion per year. The EPA had estimated that it would cost $8.5 billion per year. The EPA claimed that more stringent standards were needed in order to produce significant benefits for Americans in terms of health. However, the number of people being helped keeps changing. In November 1996 the new standards were said to have saved forty thousand Americans. In February of 1997 the amount was revised to twenty thousand lives saved. By May the number had been revised downward again to reflect a total of fifteen thousand lives saved. Meanwhile, Kay Jones, Ph.D., the top air quality adviser in the Carter administration, suggested that the figure was actually less than one thousand lives saved.

The statistics that the EPA has been heralding were produced by an American Cancer Society study. Yet the EPA refuses to release the details to the public, despite the fact that American taxpayers financed the research.[3]

The Acid Test

At times, the rush to enact environmental regulations seems devoid of any logic. For instance, in March 1980 the Senate was debating the issue of acid rain. After a lengthy discussion, a bill was proposed and it was determined that the cost of addressing the problem would range anywhere from five to ten billion dollars a year. The National Acid Precipitation Assessment Program (NAPAP) completed a ten-year scientific study on the subject of acid rain. A half billion dollars was spent on the investigation to try to deal with this problem. The NAPAP found that, despite the fact that sulfur dioxide emissions had decreased 23% and nitrogen oxides had declined 14% between 1973 and 1988, no change in the acidity of rainfall could be detected. Their conclusion was that there was no proportional relationship between cutting sulfur dioxide emissions and reducing acid rain.

The NAPAP study contradicted the claim of environmentalists that acid rain was caused only by sulfur dioxide from industrial sources. The study found that local geology and soil drainage can contribute to the acidification of rain. They also found that acid rain seems to have no effect on trees, with the exception of select species at high elevations. In fact, acid rain may even help to fertilize trees. All this information did not discourage Congress from implementing a solution. Rather than considering the NAPAP study, they chose instead to rely upon a 1983 National Academy of Science report as the basis for taking action. This report stated that there was a proportionate relationship between cutting sulfur dioxide emission and reducing acid rain.[4]

It appears as though our leaders were not seeking real answers to environmental problems. In this case, as in so many other instances, scientific principles are ignored to further what is regarded as a higher cause and, in the end, emotionalism triumphs over reason. The cumulative effect of these environmental regulations has impacted the American way of life in ways great and small. It is difficult to quantify how the emotional detachment from scientific reasoning and rational thinking has detrimentally affected society. However, as bad as domestic environmental law may seem, international environmental law is far more menacing.

International Environmental Law Is Ushered In

International legislation on the environment has grown to such an extent during the last few years that a new subject area,

International Environmental Law, has emerged in our law schools. All over the United States, law schools have begun to offer classes dedicated solely to the study of international environmental customs, treaties, and the application of law beyond the boundaries of individual countries.[5]

International environmental law had its beginnings at the 1972 Stockholm Conference on the Human Environment. Isolated treaties existed prior to 1972, but they were not yet in the form of an organized set of regulations at the international level. The action plan that was generated at the Stockholm conference actually laid the groundwork for future environmental treaties. Prior to the Stockholm conference, a multitude of books painted dismal pictures predicting the scarcity of natural resources, the overgrowth of population, and the pollution of air and water. Some of the more pessimistic works included *Silent Spring* (1964),[6] written by Rachel Carson, and *The Closing Circle: Nature, Man, and Technology* (1971),[7] written by Barry Commoner. A flurry of proposals about a frail earth sowed the seeds of fear in the minds of sympathetic listeners throughout the world community. The secretary general of the Stockholm conference was that previously discussed well-known figure, Maurice Strong.

The Stockholm conference resulted in the creation of the United Nations Environmental Program (UNEP). UNEP coordinates activities among different countries and agencies and works to promote initiatives involving global ecology and sustainable development. It often establishes partnerships with other UN agencies, NGOs, and private businesses. UNEP is the entity that maintains information systems, such as the Global Environmental Monitoring System (GEMS). It has been intimately involved in the creation of many treaties, including the Biodiversity Convention and the Montreal Protocol.

United Nations Convention on the Law of the Sea

Before the Stockholm conference had even taken place, negotiations for the Law of the Sea had already started. The United Nations Law of the Sea (UNCLOS)[8] has been called "the most ambitious and comprehensive treaty of all times."[9] The treaty, opened for signature in 1982, came into force in November 1994. It is a far-reaching, comprehensive treaty with a total of 320 provisions, 59 of which involve environmental regulations. It is a code of international rules that applies to the oceans. Since oceans occupy over seventy percent of the earth, it is a key piece of international legislation that contributes to immense global control.

In 1982 one hundred seventeen countries took the first step toward multilateral codification of the treaty as international law. All of the countries signed the treaty. The important next step in the treaty process is ratification by each of the individual countries. The United States rejected ratification of this treaty in the past. It establishes another international bureaucracy, the International Seabed Authority (ISA). If the treaty were ratified, the United States would have its power and influence over seventy percent of the earth limited to one vote in ISA. The U.S. would have no more control than Iraq or Panama over the resources of the ocean. ISA decisions would be in the hands of Third World nations that not only harbor animosity toward the U.S., but rarely contribute to the scientific advances that allow the wealth of the ocean to be tapped. Those American enterprises that possess the financial and technological wherewithal to engage in oceanic mining would find the fruits of their labors confiscated by ISA and transferred to the UN.

Soft Law

It should be noted that when the attendees of UN conferences create a non-legally binding document, it is referred to as *soft law*. Soft law is a roadmap to future binding law for those who create it. Calling an agreement non-binding makes it easier for organizers to obtain signatures from a greater number of nations. This is merely a sales maneuver. Incremental progress is wholly acceptable to global activists. The execution of non-binding documents opens the door for other policies to be steadily promoted. Also, once the non-binding documents are signed, they can be characterized as the embodiment of international consensus. International consensus takes advantage of a bandwagon mentality. If all other countries of the world are in agreement on the provisions of a particular document, it can be a powerful lobbying tool for countries that are in support of the agreement. It is the hope and plan of organizers of conferences that produce soft law to have all, or even a portion, of the soft law evolve into a binding treaty or legislation over time.

Non-governmental organizations have become established participants in the implementation of international law. According to UN literature, NGOs allow people of the world to share in the process. Supposedly, NGOs act as our representatives. In reality, however, they are lobbyists within international organizations.

Rio Writes the Rules

In June 1992 Rio de Janeiro, Brazil, hosted the United Nations Conference on Environment and Development (UNCED), popularly called "the Earth Summit." Over 180 countries and 100 heads of state attended. Prior to leading the U.S. delegation to the Earth Summit, President Clinton urged world leaders to attend, stating, "Together we need to affirm the spirit of Rio." In an echo of almost every UN document and speech, Mr. Clinton added, "We are trying to make preservation of the environment and sustainable development the policy of every nation in the world."[10]

The following key international documents sprang from this conference:

1) the Rio Declaration on Environment and Development;
2) Agenda 21;
3) the Non-Legally Binding Authoritative Statement of Principles for a Global Consensus on the Management, Conservation, and Sustainable Development of All Types of Forests;
4) the Framework Convention on Climate Change;
5) the Biodiversity Convention.

The secretary general of the Earth Summit was the omnipresent Maurice Strong. Strong has consistently been one of the most powerful figures on the international scene. It was a forewarning of sorts when, twenty years ago, the *New Yorker* magazine described Maurice Strong as the man upon whom "the survival of civilization in something like its present form might depend." Strong has complained that "the United States is clearly the greatest risk to the world's ecological health," and he has forcefully advocated a new economic order based on the redistribution of the developed world's industries and wealth to the Third World.[11]

Among his many credentials, Strong is also a member of the UN-funded Commission on Global Governance. This body's 1995 report, *Our Global Neighborhood*,[12] contained a number of menacing proposals that included the establishment of a global tax, UN control over global commons, expansion of the powers of the World Bank, expansion of the jurisdiction of the International Court, removal of the United States veto power in the Security Council, and creation of an Economic Security Council to oversee the world's economy. Environmental concerns are major themes in the *Report of the Commission on Global Governance*. Fourteen environmental treaties are cited, beginning in 1946 and ending in 1992 with the Convention on Climate Change.[13]

The report recommends that governments should adopt policies that make maximum use of environmental taxes.[14] It notes that one of the outcomes of the Earth Summit was the creation of a Commission on Sustainable Development. This commission is an international bureaucracy consisting of fifty-two members who push sustainable development and try to implement the global agenda that was agreed to at the Rio Summit. The grand plan of the Rio Summit is Agenda 21. In order to move this agenda forward, the United Nations must have money. This is why environmental taxes, user fees, and other market instruments are being sought. Besides global taxes, another plan to raise money is a method called tradable permits. Companies would be required to pay for permits if their emissions went above a specified level. By this point, you can probably guess who would be responsible for setting the specified level. A United Nations commission has already captured that authority.[15]

The proposals of the Commission on Global Governance are intended to move us toward the creation of a world government infrastructure. Unfortunately, the unfolding of this scenario necessitates and precipitates the decline of U.S. sovereignty.

Closer to the Goal

The internationalists came out of the Earth Summit two steps closer to their dreams of global governance. The first step involved the 1992 United Nations Framework Convention on Climate Change (UNFCCC),[16] which was a treaty that sought to stabilize greenhouse gas concentrations at levels that would prevent interference with the climate. The UNFCCC created a

set of guidelines for future agreement concerning global warming. It was adopted in New York in May of 1992, and was
presented at the United Nations Conference on Environment
and Development in June of the same year. The convention
entered into force in March 1994. It set the levels of emissions,
which were used to negotiate the Climate Control Treaty (also
known as the Global Warming Treaty), signed in Kyoto, Japan.
The second step was the crafting of the Biodiversity Treaty.
Although President George Bush refused to sign this document,
President Clinton executed it. The Clinton administration lobbied for its ratification in 1994. The ratification was narrowly
rejected due to an investigative education campaign conducted by
a small handful of opponents to globalism. (The details on the
policies of this treaty and how they are being implemented despite ratification failure are set forth in Chapter Thirteen.) To
follow up on the Earth Summit, a five-day conference known as
Rio+5, was held in New York City. More than three thousand
delegates from 170 countries got together with the usual international environmental activists, ostensibly to review the progress
since the Earth Summit. After five days, the delegates emerged
with a 200,000-word blueprint in which the term sustainable
development was used over and over again. One of their primary
purposes was to set up a negotiation posture for the upcoming
Kyoto Summit.

     After this New York conference, spokespersons for the United
Nations approached the press with their heads hung low. The
Associated Press released stories saying that the conditions of the
earth were much worse than anyone who had attended the 1992
Earth Summit ever imagined. The attendees of the New York
meeting had warned that our oceans, forests, and the planet's
very existence were endangered. Naturally, they came to the conclusion that more money and more regulations at the international level were needed to rectify things. They also decided that
developing nations should be exempt from any emissions standards set at the Kyoto Summit.[17] In the fall of 1997 opponents
of the Global Warming Treaty began to try to counter some of
the hysteria that environmental activists had stirred up. One of
the key things that opponents pointed out was that the treaty was
not going to be enforced on developing nations, such as China,
India, Mexico, and Indonesia. Economists predicted that having
separate standards for developed and undeveloped nations would

likely cause the migration of investment capital to undeveloped nations. This would result in a massive redistribution of world wealth. Of course, this is exactly what designers of the treaty intended to happen all along.[18]

After Vice President Al Gore signed the Global Warming Treaty in Kyoto, the White House went into full spin-control mode. As reflected in a March 1998 article in the *Washington Post*,[19] the administration forecast that the agreement would result in modest price hikes, at most, for gasoline and other fuels. It also stated that any increases would be completely offset by lower electricity bills if Congress were to pass laws that allowed utility companies to compete.

When the dust finally settled in Kyoto, the treaty basically asked western industrialized nations to restrain emissions of carbon dioxide and other gases that were believed to cause artificial global warming. If the treaty is ratified, the United States must reduce emissions to 7% below 1990 levels by the year 2012.[20] Vice President Gore did manage to negotiate the year 2008 as the effective starting date of the treaty. Apparently, he is thinking optimistically and believes that he will be finishing up a second presidential term and in the clear, just in case of negative fallout. If the standards of the Kyoto Treaty are to be met, the United States will need to cut its output of greenhouse emissions by approximately one-third, in comparison with the levels that would otherwise have existed in the year 2012. Presumably, this would be done by using one-third less oil and coal. Severe restrictions on trucks and automobiles would have to be enforced if the provisions of this treaty are implemented. Many vehicles that people currently enjoy driving, such as performance cars, sport utility vehicles, and pick-up trucks, would have to be limited. Senator Larry Craig of Idaho summarized the historical implications of the signing and promotion of the treaty in a succinct way by saying, "This is the first time an American president has allowed foreign interests to control or limit the growth of the U.S. economy."[21]

The biggest losers from the Kyoto treaty appear to be the American people. As mentioned earlier, the so-called developing nations are exempt and free to pollute at will. They are also free to entice multinational manufacturers to establish operations in their countries. European nations, who are already more energy efficient than the United States because of their use of nuclear energy, are far better equipped to meet the Kyoto requirements. One of the strongest objections to the Kyoto Treaty is that its very premise is dubious. There is tremendous disagreement within the scientific community on the theory of global warming. Even those scientists who argue that the global warming theory is a real phenomenon believe that the standards set forth in the treaty will have little or no effect in the long run, even if they are strictly enforced.

The Global Marshall Plan

It begs the question that if a treaty makes little scientific sense, causes economic harm to American citizens, and fails to produce the results that its own promoters are seeking: what are the real motives behind this plan? In his book *Earth in the Balance,*[22] Al Gore reveals the hidden agenda. One of the chapters in Mr. Gore's book is entitled "A Global Marshall Plan." In this section, Gore points out the historical basis of the plan that General George Marshall and President Harry Truman implemented to address the tremendous devastation that beset Europe after World War II.[23] Gore speculates that "most individuals now feel themselves to be a part of a truly global civilization." He then sets forth five strategic goals of this Global Marshal Plan.

Goal number one is stabilizing of world population. Under the Global Marshal Plan, policies would be developed to create changes in every nation, from high birth rates to a stable equilibrium of low birth rates and death rates.[24] Gore does not specify how this change is to take place.

Goal number two is "the rapid creation and development of environmentally appropriate technologies."[25] Gore states that these new technologies must be transferred quickly to all nations, especially Third World nations. Third World nations will not be required to pay for them in cash but can be compensated by discharging obligations they incur as participants in the Global Marshal Plan.

Goal number three is a complete change in the economic rules of the road, by which we measure the impact of our decisions on the environment.[26] According to Gore, we must establish a new economic system that assigns appropriate values to ecological consequences.

Goal number four is "the negotiation and approval of a new generation of international agreements." Gore sees more international treaties containing regulatory frameworks, specific prohibitions, and enforcement mechanisms.[27] In essence, he is talking about the creation of a global bureaucracy. The loss of sovereignty, encroachment on individual freedom, and reduction in the standard of living are just necessary sacrifices we will have to make in order to meet the global goals.

Goal number five is the establishment of a method for educating the citizenry of the world about our global environment.[28] This goal sounds like a global version of Goals 2000, using an outcome-based education approach to indoctrinate future global citizens. *The Report of the Commission on Global Governance* speaks of these same underlying goals when declaring a new definition of sovereignty. It states, "In an increasingly interdependent world, old notions of territoriality, independence, and non-intervention lose some of their meaning. National boundaries are increasingly permeable and, in some important respects, less relevant."[29]

Environmental concerns are exaggerated into crises. Science is distorted or ignored. Regulatory schemes, totally devoid of common sense, are generated at the international level because the environment is being used as a pretext to accomplish these disturbing global objectives. The underlying ideas and philosophies involved in deep ecology provide the ideal excuse for those seeking to create and strengthen international bureaucracies. The unfortunate result of this contrivance is that our sovereignty becomes dispensable and is placed in a subordinate position to the fabricated notion of a dying earth.

Notes

1. Comprehensive Environmental Response, Compensation, and Liability Act, Public Law 96-510, 42 U.S.C., Chapter 103.

2. William Tucker, "This Is No Way to Save the Earth," *Readers Digest* (June 1993).

3. Citizens for a Sound Economy press release, "EPA On Wrong Side of Science, Group Charges" (29 May 1997). Citizens for a Sound Economy Foundation, 1250 H Street, NW, #700, Washington, DC, 20005.

4. "The Answers on Acid Rain Fall on Deaf Ears," *Wall Street Journal* (6 March 1990).

5. William R. Slomanson, *Fundamental Perspectives on International Law* 2d ed. (St. Paul, MN: West, 1995), 538.

6. Rachel Carson, *Silent Spring* (New York: Fawcett Crest, 1964). The 1994 reissue of the book includes an introduction by Albert Gore.

7. Barry Commoner, *The Closing Circle: Nature, Man, and Technology* (New York: Knopf, 1971).

8. United Nations Convention on the Law of the Sea, 5 Weston V.F.22.

9. Slomanson, *Fundamental Perspectives on International Law*, 231.

10. "Pushing World 'Green' Policies, Clinton to Attend UN Environmental Summit," *Daytona Beach Florida News Journal* (10 May 1997).

11. As quoted by the *Toronto Star* (19 May 1994) in a profile of Maurice Strong.

12. The Commission on Global Governance, *Our Global Neighborhood: The Report of the Commission on Global Governance* (New York: Oxford University Press, 1995).

13. Ibid., 209. (Treaties mentioned include the Whaling Convention of 1946, the Wetlands Convention of 1971, the Convention on Marine Waste Dumping of 1972, the Convention on the International Trade in Endangered Species of 1973, the Convention on Ship Pollution of 1973, the Convention on Long-Range Transboundary Pollution of 1979, the Convention on Migratory Species of Wild Animals of 1979, the UN Law of the Sea of 1982, the International Tropical Timber Agreement of 1983, the Vienna Convention on Ozone Layer of 1985, including the Montreal Protocol of 1987, the Convention on Early Notification of Nuclear Accidents of 1986, the Convention on Transboundary Movement of Hazardous Wastes of 1989, the Biological Diversity Convention of 1992, and the Framework Convention on Climate Change in 1992.)

14. Ibid., 212.

15. Ibid., 213-214.

16. United Nations Framework Convention on Climate Change (UNFCCC). Entered into force, 21 March 1994. Can be located on the web at United Nations Environment Programme http://unep.unep.org/unep/secretar/climchng/home.htm.

17. "Earth Summit Ending on a Low Note," *The Augusta Chronicle* (27 June 1997). See also "Summit Ending on Pessimistic Note, With Last Minute Snags," *The Daytona Beach Florida News Journal* (28 June 1997).

18. "The Trade-off for Global Warming Hysteria," *Orange County Register* (7 October 1997). See also "There Is Little Support for Global Treaty," *Grand Island Independent* (9 December 1997).

19. Editorial Staff, "Hot Air and Climate Change," *Washington Post* (26 March 1998).

20. Joby Warrick, "Reassessing Kyoto Agreement, Scientists See Little Environmental Advantage," *Washington Post* (13 February 1998).

21. Editorial Staff, *Washington Post*.

22. Albert Gore, *Earth in the Balance* (Boston: Houghton Mifflin, 1992).

23. Ibid., 296-298.

24. Ibid., 305-306.

25. Ibid., 306.

26. Ibid., 306.

27. Ibid., 306.

28. Ibid., 306-307.

29. The Commission on Global Governance, *Our Global Neighborhood: The Report of the Commission on Global Governance*, 70.

Eleven

Trading Away the Constitution

The Constitution requires that treaties must be approved by a two-thirds vote of the Senate in order to be enforceable as American law. In recent years, this constitutional provision has been repeatedly ignored. The evasion of proper procedural requirements has had enormous consequences on the functioning of our government and serious effects on the discourse with the American people. The saga of manipulating events and averting the Constitution involves sophisticated public relation campaigns, and oftentimes outright duplicity, revealing the ugly underbelly of politics. If we examine the many cumulative compromises that have been made over time, we could easily find ourselves paraphrasing the popular old song, "How'd we ever get this way?"

The Questionable Passage of NAFTA

Abbreviated references such as GATT, NAFTA, and WTO have become familiar to most Americans. The news media provide reports about free trade when there is a debate among politicians, but the details presented are usually scant. The public has not been given the complete and proper picture when it comes to these international agreements.

On 20 November 1993 the Senate voted on a treaty called the North American Free Trade Agreement (NAFTA).[1] The Senate approved it by a vote of sixty-one to thirty-eight, but a perplexing question lingers to this day. Since NAFTA was passed with less than two-thirds of the Senate present, how could it possibly be valid under the Constitution?[2] After a long and heated discussion of pertinent issues, why was there no mention of this constitutional concern? Considering the fact that thirty-eight senators voted against NAFTA, and numerous high profile leaders sought the demise of the treaty, it would seem as if any and all arguments would have been used in an attempt to defeat the measure. Evidently, the political and legal elite accepted this new kind of approval procedure as unassailable. What is unfortunate for the American people is that this procedure cannot be reconciled with the provisions of the Constitution.

Antics with Legal Semantics

The question of whether a world trade agreement can be passed with less than a two-thirds majority so plagued the community of scholars that, in 1995, a book-length article about NAFTA, written by Bruce Ackerman, Professor of Law at Yale, and David Golove, Professor of Law at the University of Arizona, appeared in the prestigious *Harvard Law Review*. The article was entitled "Is NAFTA Constitutional?"[3] After one hundred twenty-four pages of discussion, the two professors came to the conclusion that NAFTA was valid, but it appeared as though they were arguing with the very essence of the Constitution and the real intent of the framers.

When the framers held the Constitutional Convention of 1787, they intentionally excluded the House of Representatives from being involved with treaty making. After debating the matter, they felt that foreign relations needed a discreet quality, such as that of the smaller senatorial body. At that time, the Senate consisted of only twenty-six senators from thirteen colonies. The framers did not feel they had to define the word "treaty." In their world, it was a generic word that referred to any form of international agreement between nations. For 150 years after the country was established, a binding obligation between nations could never even have been considered enforceable without the required two-thirds vote of the Senate.[4]

In 1945 a constitutional amendment was drafted to modify the approval process required for a treaty to be valid. The proposed amendment would have allowed treaties to be fully enforceable law if approved by majorities in both Houses rather than by the traditional two-thirds vote of the Senate. However, the movement to promote the establishment of this new amendment became unnecessary, primarily because of a novel manipulation of legal semantics. Through undue expansion of a simple term called "executive agreement," a new approval procedure was utilized, despite the fact that it did not appear anywhere in the Constitution.

Foundations of Treaty Making

The framers of the Constitution debated the treaty making power vigorously. Both Madison and Hamilton believed that treaty making was a legislative function rather than an executive role. Hamilton noted that the King of England could make treaties by himself, and he certainly did not want the president to be compared with the British sovereign from whom this young country had just broken away. "In this respect, therefore, there is no comparison between the intended power of the President and the actual power of the British sovereign."[5] Hamilton's language indicates that he regarded the two-thirds approval requirement of the Senate to be mandatory for every possible international agreement.

One of the delegates to the Constitutional Convention, Roger Sherman, made a statement about the treaty power in relation to international agreements. He said that the Senate and the president "ought to act jointly in every transaction with respect to the business of negotiation with foreign powers."[6] Hamilton also believed that the treaty clause was one of the "best digested and unexceptionable parts of the plan." He thought that it was "utterly unsafe and improper to entrust that power to an elective magistrate of four years duration."[7]

Without a doubt, the writers of the Constitution would have been shocked to find out that trade agreements such as NAFTA, GATT, and the WTO would be characterized as anything but treaties. In 1796 there was great debate over the Jay Treaty with England. The House demanded access from President George Washington to all official papers connected with the negotiation of this treaty. When Washington refused to give these official papers to the House of Representatives, he stated, "The power of making treaties is exclusively vested in the President, by and with the Advice and Consent of the Senate."[8] The approval process for treaties is described in the Constitution by the phrase that Washington used, "the Advice and Consent of the Senate."[9] By employing these words, Washington confirmed his belief and support for the constitutional provision that requires a two-thirds vote by the Senate before a treaty is valid. The feud about treaty power continued over time, but the description embodied in the Constitution was honored for the next 150 years.

Presidential power encompasses some limited international agreements. For example, the president has the power to negotiate a cease-fire or grant a pardon. However, one can search the Constitution from beginning to end and not find any mention of the term executive agreement. Nowhere in the Constitution is independent power granted to the president to make international agreements. In cases where there is time for the Senate to act and where an agreement has importance in foreign relations, it is clear that the constitutional requirement of two-thirds approval of the Senate must be followed.

The Treaty Power and the New Deal

The 1930s brought about President Roosevelt's New Deal. Because of the Great Depression, economic policy was paramount. Two agreements involving specific commodities were inaugurated. One was the Silver Agreement of 1933 and the other was the Wheat Agreement of 1933. Both of these agreements had international implications. Yet President Roosevelt did not submit either agreement to the Senate. Instead, he declared these international initiatives to be executive agreements. He simply placed them into law via a proclamation, believing that a previous act of Congress, the Agricultural Adjustment Act of 1933, gave him the power to do so. No opposing argument was mounted, and, after all, these actions were viewed as emergency measures in desperate times.

In 1934 President Roosevelt began to pursue broader international trade initiatives. One such initiative was called the Reciprocal Trade Agreements Act of 1934. Roosevelt felt that the existing procedure for approving treaties was too slow to meet the economic challenges of his time. He sought his own version of what today we call fast track, an authorization by Congress to enter into a legally binding international trade agreement. Congress gave Roosevelt this ability, with overwhelming majorities in both Houses. Any criticism invoking the Constitution was easily suppressed due to the exigent circumstances of post-depression times. Thus, a constitutional aberration was allowed to take place. The president had always had the power, in very limited categories, to bind our nation. These specific instances had to do with military matters and settlement of claims. However, in the era of the New Deal, presidential authority was stretched out of proportion, permitting the president to enter into binding international agreements with a prior authorization of Congress.

It takes some historical recall and empathy to understand the mood of the nation and the collective mindset of the American people during these intensely turbulent times. In 1936 the Senate failed to approve the Treaty of Versailles and the public began to question the need for a two-thirds approval by the Senate. In October 1943 it was such a major issue that a Gallup poll was taken to gauge public opinion as to whether or not the two-thirds majority of the Senate needed for approving treaties should be retained. Fifty-four percent of those surveyed thought that a simple majority in both Houses should be the new rule. By May 1944 the percentage of people favoring a change to a majority vote in both Houses had risen to sixty percent.[10]

Because of public sentiment, a constitutional amendment was finally proposed and formally approved by the House of Representatives to change the Constitution to eliminate the two-thirds requirement in the Senate. By 1945 Congress was not dealing with whether the Senate would lose its two-thirds approval power but was pondering how it would be changed. A number of proposed constitutional amendments were being circulated through the House of Representatives. Simultaneously, the United Nations Charter, the founding document of the United Nations, was submitted to the Senate as a treaty. The Senate approved it, partially believing that they were preserving their treaty making power for the future.

The difficulty of restoring the damaged economies of the affected nations was on the minds of world leaders after the devastation of World War II. As a result of the Bretton Wood Conference in 1944, three organizations were established: the International Trade Organization (ITO), the International Monetary Fund (IMF), and the World Bank. Because the Senate refused to ratify the ITO, it emerged in 1947 as the General Agreement on Tariffs and Trade (GATT).[11] Since these important organizations were established in the conference, and have been influential over the world economy ever since, they were referred to as the Bretton Woods Regime.[12]

This establishment of the World Bank and the International Monetary Fund created a whole new international economic order. Rather than confronting these major issues head on, the weak-spirited Senate of 1945 approved both broad, sweeping international agreements. A trickle of executive agreements turned into a waterfall with Roosevelt pushing through one international agreement after another. The proliferation of treaties led to the campaign to amend the Constitution by Senator Bricker, as set forth in Chapter 6. Early versions of the Bricker amendment contained a provision that specified executive agreements could not be made in lieu of treaties.[13]

By this time, legal scholars fully embraced the loophole of using a two-House approval for treaties, as long as they were labeled executive agreements. Professor Louis Henkin of Columbia University explained his view of the bypass of the Constitution when he said:

> Whatever theoretical merits, it is now widely accepted that the Congressional-executive agreement is a complete alternative to a treaty: the President can seek approval of any agreement by joint resolution of both Houses of Congress instead of two-thirds of the Senate only. Like a treaty, such an agreement is the law of the land superseding inconsistent state laws as well as inconsistent provisions in earlier treaties, other international agreements, or acts of Congress.[14]

By making it easier for a treaty to become the supreme law of the land, a greater opportunity to erode state sovereignty and individual liberties exists, thereby empowering government to more readily implement international bureaucracy.

A Faster Track to Unconstitutional Approval

The Trade Act of 1974[15] created the famous fast track procedure to further expedite the approval of world trade pacts. In using this approach, Congress delegates authority to the president to negotiate within pre-approved parameters. Ultimately, Congress's involvement is limited to a "yea" or "nay" vote without amendments, once the international agreement is presented. The very same fast track procedure was used to negotiate and approve NAFTA. The WTO[16] is the most recent addition to a collection of international trade pacts that fail to conform to the Constitution. This executive agreement was passed in 1995 as part of the Uruguay Round of the new GATT.[17] (It is referred to as the "new GATT" to distinguish it from the original GATT of 1947.) The documents associated with this agreement consist of more than twenty-six thousand pages. As is true of all of these world trade pacts, it is an exhaustingly comprehensive and pervasive multilateral treaty, as defined by the Constitution.

Coalitions Make Strange Bedfellows

Since creation of the WTO treaty threatened to produce significant erosion of American sovereignty, some unusual coalitions formed to oppose it. Individuals expressing objections included such distant political cohorts as Senator Jesse Helms, Ralph Nader, Patrick Buchanan, and Harvard Law Professor Lawrence Tribe. Although those in opposition to the WTO gently raised the constitutional issue discussed above, proponents of the treaty effectively suppressed the argument. The WTO is, in essence, a gigantic economic Supreme Court. One of its primary functions is to preside over international mandatory dispute resolution. Complicated rules of procedure and practice that are found in most jurisdictions or courts in the Western world are also contained within the regulations for the dispute resolution function of the WTO. The international community was extremely pleased with one of the key elements of this new treaty. Under the WTO, the most powerful economy in the world, the United States, had significantly reduced its influence and power. Under the old GATT, dispute resolution procedures were not truly binding on the United States. A nation in GATT could pick and choose which provisions of the various agreements it deemed applicable. The new WTO agreement required that each of the participating nations agree to all of the basic provisions.

The old GATT limited its application to commodities. The WTO encompasses goods, services, intellectual properties, and investments. Any country that is a party to the WTO and is unhappy about a trade practice in which the United States is engaging can file an action with the WTO that is the equivalent of a lawsuit. If the United States loses (and at the international level the United States is not favored to win any proceeding) the United States must seek review by the WTO's appellate body in Geneva. As a result, there is a complete surrender of American sovereignty to the WTO. Furthermore, the United States has a vote equal to every other member in the WTO. This means that, effectively, the voting power of the United States is reduced to the same level as that of Angola, Peru, Egypt, or Mongolia.[18]

WTO and the Venezuelan Controversy

In one of the first cases presented to the WTO, Venezuela filed a complaint because environmental standards of the United States required cleaner oil than the Venezuelans were producing. Those at the WTO holding antipathy toward America could not wait to render a decision that the United States and its citizens would be forced to obey.

On 25 March 1995 Venezuela filed the formal equivalent of a lawsuit with the WTO's Dispute Settlement Body (DSB).[19] The defendant in this complaint was the United States. Venezuela alleged that the United States had violated GATT by virtue of environmental regulations that set forth standards for gasoline. Brazil filed a similar action in May of the same year. Since these other nations were filing, the European community and Norway joined in. Our EPA rules were an attempt to reduce air contaminants in nine urban areas throughout the United States. Venezuela and Brazil were charging that the regulations gave foreign refiners less favorable treatment than domestic ones. The United States disputed this contention by saying that it treated all refiners the same, and the rules were intended to improve air quality throughout the United States. The WTO Dispute Settlement Body in January of 1996 found the United States in violation of GATT, asserting that the United States had discriminated against foreign gasoline producers.[20] The United States appealed the decision and in April 1996, the WTO's appellate body heard its first case. The appellate body predictably agreed with the lower panel, determining that the United States gasoline rule discriminated against foreign gasoline producers. This was an important test regarding the manner in which the WTO would operate. It clearly illustrated the tremendous loss of American sovereignty the new treaty had wrought. In this case, the WTO thwarted the legitimate environmental concerns of the American people.

Fast Track: The Hidden Track Record

In 1997 a series of television advertisements appeared that were designed to help promote the passage of fast track trade legislation. The ads referred to "new Democrats leading the way as America builds a new economy." Nowhere to be found were the terms NAFTA or WTO. Members of the administration publicly joked that they had excluded the word NAFTA from any public discourse in order to advance the cause of fast track legislation. One of the administration's primary goals in seeking negotiating authority was to extend NAFTA beyond Mexico and Canada to the rest of the western hemisphere, thus creating a new homogeneous economic region of the Americas that would encompass nearly 800 million people. The rationale for avoiding any association with the track record of these international trade agreements was obvious. There was a desire for the truth concerning the effects of these trade pacts to remain hidden from the public.

The last time Congress granted fast track authority to a sitting president, the WTO was delivered and the voting power of the U.S. was rendered equal to that of a Third World country. Although this transfer of power distressed many members of Congress, there was nothing that they could do because they had already delegated their authority to alter any agreement by granting fast track. It is predictable that the supporters of fast track would be backing away from NAFTA's ruinous track record. Due to inadequate funding, increased shipping volume, and limitations of inspections imposed by NAFTA, government systems charged with guaranteeing the safety of imported food have been overwhelmed. Fewer than one percent of the 3.3 million trucks entering the U.S. each year are inspected. In addition, reports indicate that crops designated for export to the U.S. are irrigated with untreated sewage. U.S. public health laws have been circumvented and the quality of the U.S. food supply has been imperiled with contaminated and pesticide-laden products.

Reduced inspections under NAFTA have also had the tragic effect of increasing the transport of illegal drugs into our country. Seventy percent of the cocaine coming into the U.S. is now entering our country from Mexico. It is the ultimate irony that a treaty intended to stabilize Mexico has heightened social and political disorder and created a flood of immigration. Americans were promised that NAFTA-induced prosperity would reduce illegal immigration from Mexico. Instead, the incentive to immigrate has been significantly increased. The loss of 28,000 small businesses and two million jobs, along with a real wage drop of twenty percent, have encouraged many Mexicans to continue to seek employment in the United States, despite NAFTA.

The trade deficit results are equally catastrophic. A U.S.

surplus with Mexico of $1.7 billion in 1993 became a deficit of $16.2 billion in 1996. America's overall deficit with NAFTA participants hit $39 billion in 1996, an increase of 332%. Portions of our agricultural industry have been irreparably reduced. This increase in the trade deficit has caused the loss of 420,000 jobs in the United States.[21] The 1995 peso crisis is commonly used to excuse the decline of the U.S. trade balance with Mexico. However, Mexico intentionally depreciated the peso in order to attract direct foreign investment and export-oriented manufacturing. The devalued peso was a deliberate act of manipulation perpetrated by a corrupt government regime.

Our founding fathers acknowledged the existence of evil within and outside our borders. This notion was originally expressed in the religious concept of a fallen world. The imperfect nature of human beings required that a government be designed to prevent the undue consolidation of power in any one branch or any single individual. Limited government, one that derives its power from the people pursuant to a legal grant of authority, was developed specifically for this purpose.

This view is in sharp contrast to the perspective held by those desirous of a homogenized, world, social, and economic system. Those seeking a global structural order believe that the imperfections of humankind can be remedied only if the correct world system is implemented. The attempted merger of all of the disparate cultures of North and South America for alleged economic purposes is therefore proposed without regard for the relative moral differences among the respective countries.

The idea that we might pass judgment or strongly disagree with governments and individuals whose values and assumptions differ radically from our own is a forbidden notion due to what has, however vaguely and imprecisely, become known as multiculturalism. In an attempt to avoid being nationalistic or ethnocentric, valuable state interests are given away freely and cheaply. Ideas like patriotism, autonomy, and national identity are shunned by our side but embraced by those with whom we bargain.

To this day, we still hear unwarranted criticism of the famous statement of Ronald Reagan that correctly designated the Soviet Union as an evil empire. Corrupt regimes must be identified and treated as such for the purposes of international policy.

The American people cannot allow their duly elected representatives to fritter away the authority and obligation to scrutinize the expansion of global economics in this hemisphere. If the Constitution were rewritten today, the treaty clause might be worded differently. If those promoting a global economy wish to amend the Constitution, they should go about doing so in the proper way through the appropriate methods. Merely renaming an international initiative as an executive agreement does not nullify the constitutional requirement to obtain two-thirds Senate approval.

Notes

1. North American Free Trade Agreement between the Government of Canada, the Government of the United Mexican States, and the Government of the United States of America. Posted on the Organization of American States web site. http://www.sice.oas.org/trade/nafta/naftatce.stm.

2. United States Constitution, Article II, Section 2.

3. Bruce Ackerman and David Golove, "Is NAFTA Constitutional?" *Harvard Law Review*, 108, No. 4, (February 1995), 799.

4. Ibid., 802.

5. Alexander Hamilton, *The Federalist* (No. 69), 467-68, Jacob E. Cooke, ed. (Middletown, CT: Wesleyan University Press, 1961) as quoted by Michael J. Glennon, *Constitutional Diplomacy* (Princeton, NJ: Princeton University Press, 1990), 182.

6. Michael J. Glennon, *Constitutional Diplomacy* (Princeton, NJ: Princeton University Press, 1990), 182.

7. Ibid., 183.

8. Ackerman and Golove, *Harvard Law Review*, 811.

9. United States Constitution, Article II, Section 2.

10. Ackerman and Golove, *Harvard Law Review*, 863.

11. General Agreement on Tariffs and Trade. Concluded at Geneva, 30 October 1947. Entered into force (provisionally) 1 January 1948. Reprinted in 4 Weston IV.C.1.

12. Bryan Johnson, ed. "Bretton Woods Revisited: GATT," *Political Economy* (27 February 1998). http://www.suite101.com/articles/article.cfm/5861.

13. Ibid., 98.

14. Louis Henkin, *Foreign Affairs and the Constitution* (Westbury, NY: Foundation Press, 1972), 175.

15. 19 U.S.C. 2432.

16. The World Trade Organization Home Page. http://www.wto.org.

17. General Agreement on Tariffs and Trade (1994). Entered into force, 1 January 1995. Reprinted in 4 Weston IV.C.2b.

18. See "GATT and the Resolution of International Trade Disputes," International Contract Adviser, II, No. 1 (Winter, 1996).

19. Understanding on Rules and Procedures Governing the Settlement of Disputes. Entered into force, 1 January 1995. Reprinted in 4 Weston IV.C.3.

20. William Buckley, "WTO Ruling against U.S. Is No Cause for Tantrum," *The Salt Lake Tribune* (26 January 1996).

21. James Hirsen, "Fast Track: The Hidden Track Record," *Covenant Syndicate*, 1, No. 56 (3 November 1997). http://capo.org/opeds/fasttrak.html.

Twelve

The Clandestine Disarmament

There have been a number of disturbing trends in the military in recent years, but the idea of putting our sons' and daughters' lives on the line for a foreign commander is one of the most repugnant. Once more, we find that the international bureaucrats have been busily working behind the scenes. Their intention concerning the military is to engulf the combat prowess of the United States and appropriate it to the United Nations.

New Military Policies, New Problems

The policy regarding U.S. forces being placed under the command of the United Nations collided with one patriotic and courageous individual when it met up with Army Specialist Michael New. On 21 August 1995 Michael New learned that before being deployed to Macedonia, members of the U.S. Army Third Infantry Division had been ordered to wear the blue uniforms, blue berets, and shoulder badges bearing the insignia of the United Nations. New had taken an oath upon entering the army in 1993 which read: *I do solemnly swear that I will support and defend the Constitution of the United States against all enemies, foreign and domestic; that I will bear true faith and allegiance to the same; and that I will obey the orders of the President of the United States and the orders of the officers appointed over me, according to regulations and the Uniform Code of Military Justice. So help me God.*[1] Specialist New asked for a written explanation regarding the unprecedented order to assume a UN uniform. The response came that the order was a direct command from the president of the United States. New told his superior that he had taken an oath to the United States Constitution and could not find in his oath or in the Constitution any reference to the United Nations. New's ultimate concerns were that if he could be forced to wear the UN attire overseas, he could be forced to wear such foreign regalia within America's borders at some future date, perhaps even against his own countrymen.

On Tuesday, 10 October 1995, Michael New refused to assemble dressed in the uniform of the United Nations. Five hundred fifty soldiers stood at attention that day, and only one was dressed in a United States uniform. That lone soldier was Army Specialist Michael New, a medic and decorated veteran of Desert Storm. He was twenty-two years old at the time. New was court-martialed for refusing to comply with this order. The army pursued a bad conduct discharge against New, despite the fact that he was willing to be discreetly moved to another unit. No American soldier has ever been court-martialed for refusing to wear a foreign government's uniform. As a matter of fact, military law forbids foreign emblems, insignias, or uniforms to be worn by a member of the United States armed forces. The United Nations is treated as a foreign government in all domestic legal matters. The building that houses its headquarters is often considered a separate sovereign domain. Moreover, the question of the constitutionality of such an order is sufficiently muddled to provide an additional defense in Specialist New's case.

When word of Michael New's court-martial in Germany arrived back home, U.S. Representative James A. Traficant, Jr. introduced a resolution condemning the court-martial. He was joined by U.S. Representative Roscoe Bartlett. Bartlett pointed out that Specialist New was willing to serve in Macedonia with his unit, but was merely refusing to wear the blue beret and shoulder badge of the United Nations. The resolution pointed out that Congress must approve the participation of the United States armed forces in UN deployment. The resolution also noted that U.S. law prohibits members of the armed forces from wearing badges or insignia from a foreign government. Therefore, the army's action, in compelling Michael New to wear the UN insignia on his uniform, was unconstitutional. Traficant summed it up by saying, "Michael New is an American hero, and I will continue to do everything I can to reverse his conviction and to ensure that no American soldier is ever forced to wear a foreign uniform again."[2]

The military judge in charge of the court-martial of Specialist New refused to hear any of the evidence concerning the illegality of the order. New was ultimately convicted by a court-martial jury in 1996 and sentenced to a bad-conduct discharge, which is being held in abeyance pending his military appeals.

New looked to the federal courts for a judicial review but was rejected by the federal trial court and the U.S. Circuit Court of Appeals for the District of Columbia. The appeals court ruled in November 1997 that New is barred from seeking a judicial review because he has not completed the appeals of his conviction with the military justice system. In March 1998 the Supreme Court cast aside New's argument that he is entitled to an honorable discharge.[3]

Michael New is a committed Christian and a man of outstanding moral courage. Throughout his ordeal, he received a tremendous amount of encouragement from the public. He was showered with thousands of letters and even had the support of many people in government. He is now on involuntary leave in the Houston area.[4] Meanwhile, there are eight sponsors to House Congressional Resolution 158 (H.C.R. 158), which is a continuation of the original resolution proposed by Representatives Bartlett and Traficant. The resolution would make it illegal to force Americans to serve under the United Nations.

The NATO Shuffle

The idea of American military personnel serving under the United Nations surfaced when U.S. soldiers were killed in Iraq. At the time, Vice President Al Gore told the friends and families of these dead soldiers that they could be proud that their loved ones had died in the service of the United Nations.[5] This starkly illustrated the beliefs of many members in the Clinton administration. They harbored a desire to integrate American armed forces with the United Nations "Peace Army."

When the Cold War ended, there was a vestige from the days of the old Soviet threat that remained with us. This remnant entity goes by the name of the North Atlantic Treaty Organization (NATO).[6] To those old enough to enjoy a perspective on this notable period of history, NATO is no less than a dinosaur, a relic from another era. It should have passed away with dignity, like the Berlin Wall or *Pravda*. Instead, it has been kept on life support by the UN and by businesses such as the defense industry that stand to benefit from its propagation. In the past, NATO served a number of historical functions. Its purposes can be traced back to the Cold War notion of keeping the Russians out of

Europe and preventing Germany from reasserting dangerous power. Confronting the Soviet Union in Europe was central to NATO's purpose. Because of this role, NATO still has an anti-Russian quality about it. This is precisely why Poland and the Czech Republic want to join, and this is exactly why Russia does not want to see NATO expand. To compound matters, the United States is the sole remaining superpower, and, the former Soviet Union's great antagonist, Germany, is the dominant economic power on the European continent.

Broadening the powers of NATO will needlessly isolate Russia. It is not prudent policy to foment an atmosphere of insecurity in a country that retains a sizable nuclear arsenal. By augmenting an obsolete military alliance, such as NATO, we could be unwittingly contributing to the creation of a forceful adversary. In the case of Bosnia, U.S. armed forces were put under NATO authority rather than being designated for placement under the control of the United Nations. This was done to stem the criticism against placing American servicemen and women under UN command. As of this writing, our troops are still in Bosnia, in a seemingly never-ending peacekeeping venture. Assigning troops to NATO command is part of a broader expansion plan of international officials. NATO expansion would allow American armed forces to be installed under foreign command over and over again, without having to obtain permission from Congress. The preamble of the North Atlantic Treaty declares allegiance to the United Nations Charter with the words: *The Parties to this Treaty reaffirm their faith in the purposes and principles of the Charter of the United Nations . . .*[7]

On 8 July 1997, at the Madrid Summit, President Clinton formally invited Poland, Hungary, and the Czech Republic to join NATO. Since one of the main purposes of NATO was to protect Europe against a belligerent Communist dictatorship, and that purpose no longer exists, we must question why we are making NATO larger as potential enemies are getting smaller. The answer lies in the global agenda of the internationalists. Article 5 of the North Atlantic Treaty requires each NATO member to "agree that an armed attack against one or more of them in Europe or North America shall be considered an attack against them all."[8] This severely impairs Congress's constitutional authority to autonomously declare war, while at the same time, NATO members have a guarantee of U.S. military protection should they require it. What this means is that we would have to go to war, up to and including nuclear conflict, to defend every member nation in NATO, whether or not we feel U.S. interests are at stake. Many of the potential new member nations are small, unstable European countries. They frequently have a long history of ethnic, national, religious, and territorial hostility. In reality, NATO expansion ends up weakening American national security rather than strengthening it. Our country, and particularly the men and women of our military, are placed in greater and greater jeopardy as these expansion plans are fulfilled.

When senators inquired about whether the cost of upgrading the defensive strength of these former Communist states would be too expensive, the Clinton administration replied in a contradictory way, saying that because there is no real threat, the expansion will be inexpensive. However, logic dictates that, if there is no real threat, then there is no real need to expand NATO at all. If the more undeveloped countries of Eastern Europe such as Romania, Slovenia, Slovakia, and the Baltic republics, are bought into the NATO fold, the cost of upgrading their respective militaries could be astronomical. This will be in addition to the tens of billions of dollars we are paying every year to maintain over 100,000 troops in Europe, and an untold number of forces on various peacekeeping missions.

The Clinton administration announced that consideration will also be given to asking Romania, Slovenia, the Baltic states, Austria, and Bulgaria to join NATO in another two years.[9] Adding Hungary, Poland, and the Czech Republic to NATO again provides little or no benefit to the United States. The addition will further undermine national security by overextending military commitments. Congressional and Pentagon reports indicate that U.S. military readiness is on the wane due to overextended overseas deployments that have taken place.[10] There is an untenable confiscatory characteristic in the way in which money is being allocated and sacrifices are continually being demanded of our citizens. On 30 April 1998, after a heated debate, the United States Senate ratified the expansion of NATO to include Poland, Czechoslovakia, and Hungary.[11]

Better Losing through Chemistry

In April of 1997 the Senate ratified another one of the many treaties coming out of the United Nations treaty factory. Ostensibly, the Chemical Weapons Convention[12] was supposed to ban chemical weapons, thereby promoting peace in the world. However, nations that have demonstrated by past actions that they were likely to utilize such horrific weapons either refused to execute the treaty or indicated that they did not consider it enforceable. These nations include Iraq, Syria, North Korea, Libya, Iran, China, and Russia. United States intelligence organizations suggested, in reports to the Senate, that compliance with this treaty could not be verified. Under circumstances such as these, the Chemical Weapons Treaty is just another piece of international legislation in which our country's participation makes no sense. It forces the United States to cease developing or financing chemical warfare, while potential adversaries continue to produce and improve upon such weaponry.

Iraq will undoubtedly continue to manufacture and utilize chemical weapons. Contrary to public statements by the United States and Iraq, such weapons appear to have already been used by Iraq during the Gulf War. One of the major problems with this type of ban is that many of the substances that are used as ingredients in chemical weapons can also be employed for non-military, industrial purposes. Therefore, it is practically impossible to exclude all potentially dangerous chemicals. The pragmatic effect of such a treaty is that it requires the U.S. to transfer sophisticated chemical weapons production and defensive technology to rogue nations, the ones most likely to use it for hostile purposes.

In addition, this treaty, like so many others, creates a bureaucracy at the international level. Of course, any facility in question will have to be inspected to determine whether offending substances are being stored. This, again, will place a great burden on American taxpayers to fund the program. It is estimated that it will cost approximately $200 million per year to maintain. UN inspectors will be able to search private areas of American businesses, and perhaps even individual homes. To make matters worse, the treaty creates a host of mindless regulations that will affect U.S. commerce in a detrimental way. The organization that is likely to intrude upon our lives is called "The Organization for the Prohibition of Chemical Weapons." It is presently located in The Hague.[13]

This marks the first time in the history of the United States that private industry will be subject to foreign inspection. The cost of doing business will increase and expenses will inevitably be passed on to consumers. Needless to say, the paperwork will be staggering. Inspections of private property normally require probable cause under the Fourth and Fifth Amendments of the Constitution.[14] According to Judge Robert H. Bork, these constitutional prohibitions will not apply. Bork wrote a letter to Senate Judiciary Committee Chairman Orrin Hatch explaining, "A foreign state will have the right to challenge inspection of the U.S. facility without the grounds that are essential for its search warrant."[15] Once again, the familiar cadre of international bureaucrats is trampling on another set of our constitutional rights. When the United Nations sets up the monitoring authority to enforce these international agreements, sensitive intelligence information from the United States will be given away. Obviously, it is not in the best interests of the United States to entrust sensitive intelligence to UN globalists who have repeatedly shown an outright disdain for the American way of life.

A Force of Its Own

Ultimately, the United Nations wants to have its very own armed forces. Perhaps the UN is impatient since not enough of the military of the United States has been surrendered to UN command. In the previously-mentioned four-hundred-page *Report of the Commission on Global Governance*,[16] the genesis of such a military body is presented. "This underlines the need for a highly trained UN Volunteer Force that is willing, if necessary, to take combat risks to break the cycle of violence at an early stage . . . Such an international Volunteer Force would be under the exclusive authority of the Security Council and, like peace-keeping forces, under the day-to-day directions of the Secretary General."[17] This clearly describes a military force exclusively controlled by the UN with the secretary general as its venerable commander-in-chief.

In the fall of 1997 the United States secretly established a trust fund for this very purpose. An amount of $200,000 was used as seed money to create a global, standby military body for peacekeeping actions. News about the covert dealings was published in the *Washington Times* in April 1998. Sources indicated that Congress was never notified of any money transfer or of the instituting of the new trust fund. Furthermore, the State Department, hiding behind the privilege rationale, refused to produce any evidentiary documentation when asked to do so by the *Washington Times*.[18]

Ingvar Carlsson, Co-Chair of the Commission on Global Governance, and former Prime Minister of Sweden, has declared that the world's experiences in Macedonia and elsewhere provide a clear basis for reviving the concept of a UN Volunteer Force.[19] An international military force is an expensive proposition. "Maintaining a UN Volunteer Force . . . will involve expenditure probably beyond the UN's present system of government assessments. If so, this would rank high among the activities qualifying for financing under the system of automatic resources proposed in Chapter Four."[20] UN semantics have become an art form all their own. A system of automatic resources is really a global tax. Chapter Four of *Our Global Neighborhood* that the above quote cross-references has a section entitled Financing Global Governance.[21] It refers to a proposal made by Nobel-laureate James Tobin to place a tax on foreign currency transactions. This may be a prelude to some sort of a Global I.R.S. With the massive amount of money transferred electronically each day, this type of tax could provide well over $1.5 billion to the UN, annually. Quite a formidable Volunteer Force can be built up with that kind of money.

The idea of the Tobin tax was raised at a 1997 meeting of the finance ministers of the leading industrial countries of the world (Group of Seven) in Ottawa. Canadian Finance Minister Paul Martin said that he favors just such a tax on international currency transactions to provide revenue for global purposes.[22] The UN has shown that it does possess the ability to spend large amounts of money for military purposes. The UN peacekeeping budget has expanded from $700 million in 1990 to the current $3.5 billion. The UN has assessed the United States at thirty-two percent of the so-called peacekeeping budget. (Presently, U.S. law caps this expense at twenty-five percent.) Other nations, such as Russia, the United Kingdom, and France, pay less than one-fourth of what U.S. citizens have already paid.

The UN points the finger of blame at the U.S. for its supposed financial difficulty, but how is this international bureaucracy managed? The UN's annual expenditures were approximately $20 million in 1945 and have since ballooned to over $4 billion per year. The United Nations employs over 50,000 people and administers a pension plan worth approximately $15 billion. The U.S. has no voice in how this money is spent since we have no representation on the Advisory Committee on Administrative and Budgetary Questions, which makes up the UN budgets.

Military Metamorphosis

In 1961 a document entitled *Freedom From War: the United States Program for General and Complete Disarmament in a Peaceful World*[23] was published, and the task of disarming America began in earnest. This proposal called for all nations of the world to eventually turn their military structures over to the United Nations.[24] The objectives of this disarmament plan are shocking. They include: (1) the disbanding of all national armed forces and the prohibition of their reestablishment in any form other than those required to preserve internal order and for contributions to a United Nations Peace Force; (2) the elimination of all of our armaments and the means of delivering them, leaving only those that are needed for a United Nations Peace Force and for maintaining internal order; and (3) the establishment of an International Disarmament Organization to insure compliance with all disarmament obligations.[25]

In its documentation, the United Nations has consistently sought the objectives set forth in this early disarmament plan. The ultimate goal is to establish a military force that will be used to police the use of arms anywhere in the world and locate any violation of UN purposes and principles.

Article 42 of the UN Charter reads: "Should the measures provided for in Article 41 (Specified Security Council measures that do not involve military options) would [sic] be inadequate or have proved to be inadequate, it may take such action by air, sea or land forces as may be necessary to maintain or restore international peace and security."[26] When UN treaties use the language "as may be necessary," it simply means that any military action may be implemented.

Article 43 of the United Nations Charter specifically affirms the transfer of military control from the United States to the UN. "All members of the United Nations, in order to contribute to the maintenance of international peace and security, undertake to make available to the Security Council, on its call and in accordance with a special agreement or agreements, armed forces, assistance, facilities, including rights of passage, necessary for the purpose of international peace and safety."[27] This language requires our military to be ready to respond at the whim of the United Nations.[28] A United Nations Disarmament Commission is already in existence. If fully implemented, the disarmament program would place unstoppable power into the hands of the UN.

In 1994 President Clinton executed Presidential Decision Directive 25 (P.D.D. 25). The State Department released only a summary of the directive, and to this day, the actual details of P.D.D. 25 remain classified and unavailable to the public. The summary, however, sets forth the power of the president to place U.S. forces under foreign command, but there appears to be an attempt to hide this section by surrounding it with platitudinous language, as the following quote indicates:

> Defining clearly our policy regarding the command and control of American military forces in UN peace operations. The policy directive underscores the fact that the President will never relinquish command of U.S. forces. However, as Commander-in-Chief, the President has the authority to place U.S. forces under the operational control of a foreign commander when doing so serves American security interests, just as American leaders have done numerous times since the Revolutionary War, including in Operation Desert Storm. The greater the anticipated U.S. military role, the less likely it will be that the U.S. will agree to have a UN commander exercise overall operational control over U.S. forces.[29]

P.D.D. 25 was a significant step toward the creation of a UN military force. This executive order gave the president the authority to place United States military forces under the control of a foreign commander. Under President Clinton's direction, U.S. military forces participated in United Nations interventionist actions in Somalia, Macedonia, and Haiti. The signing of P.D.D.

25 also required some research, as exemplified by a Combat Arms
Survey, which, among other things, asked U.S. Marines whether
they would be willing to fire on U.S. citizens. Question number
forty-six, a true or false hypothetical, read as follows:

> The U.S. government declares a ban on the possession, sale,
> transportation, and transfer of all non-sporting firearms. A
> thirty (30) day amnesty period is permitted for these firearms
> to be turned over to the local authorities. At the end of this
> period, a number of citizen groups refuse to turn over their
> firearms. Consider the following statement: I would fire
> upon U.S. citizens who refuse or resist confiscation of
> firearms banned by the U.S. government.[30]

Learning of a survey such as this should certainly give the
average American citizen pause to wonder why members of the
United States military would be questioned as to their willingness to use force against their own citizens. The logical assumption is a terrifying one—that this option has already been discussed and perhaps even given some legitimate consideration by
our own government officials.

Preserving the Pieces

The United Nations has a patchy record when it comes to
preserving peace. Article 2, Section 4 of the UN Charter, reads:
"All members shall refrain in their international relations from
the threat or use of force against the territorial integrity or political independence of any state, or in any other manner inconsistent with the purposes of the United Nations."[31] The key language in this section is the threat or use of force against territorial
integrity. The term *aggression* is used repeatedly in UN materials
when referencing this concept. Typical of international legal documents promulgated by the United Nations, the determination of
what constitutes aggression is for the UN to decide. The Charter
notes that parties to the Charter shall not engage in a use of force
that is inconsistent with the purposes of the United Nations.
Article 39 places the power directly into the hands of the Security
Council stating, "The Security Council shall determine the existence of any threat to the peace, breach of the peace, or act of
aggression."[32] This means that the UN is the sole arbiter of whether
and when to condemn those using force against territorial integrity.

Apparently, it is this ability to decide whether or not aggression has taken place that has allowed the United Nations to look the other way when Communist nations have engaged in war crimes. The UN turned a blind eye to the Communist Chinese murder of Tibetans. When Soviet tanks invaded Hungary and Czechoslovakia, the UN stayed silent and inactive. Most recently, when numerous human rights violations occurred in Chechnya, the UN neglected to take note. The Charter also seems to be precisely what the United Nations relies upon to commit its own form of aggression.

United Nations, Inspect Yourself

In 1998 a United Nations commission completed a human rights investigation of the United States and found us to be in violation. The UN decided that our resurgence of the use of the death penalty is a breach of international law. So, a human rights investigator from the UN, Waly Bacre Ndiaye of Senegal, came to our shores to examine potential abuses. Ndiaye is a long-time UN envoy. Exploratory investigations are generally conducted in countries accused of human rights offenses. It seems that Ndiaye's trip was prompted by several allegations to a Geneva-based commission regarding an increase in U.S. executions and the likelihood of misapplications of the death penalty.

If a world body felt the necessity to explore possible human rights infringements, recorded patterns of conduct would dictate that the last place on earth to begin such an investigation would be within the American justice system. Compared to the other nations of the world, we are a virtual human rights utopia. In reality, the use of the death penalty is one of the few areas in the criminal justice system that has restored some moral, retributive, and spiritual coherence to the current upside-down climate of ours. If the UN wants to investigate human rights abuses, there is a much closer entity that needs to be scrutinized. The United Nations ought to begin with itself.

UN human rights violations are not your run of the mill atrocities. In 1993, during so-called peacekeeping operations, two UN soldiers from Belgium were charged with restraining a helpless Somali child over an open fire. Photos published by the *Village Voice*[33] showed the two soldiers smiling as they tortured the child. Another soldier is depicted forcing a child to drink worms mixed with vomit, while one more shows a UN garbed warrior urinating on the body of a presumably dead Somali victim. One might wonder if this kind of activity is rare and unusual for this conspicuous international organization. Unfortunately, the answer is no. Recent UN peacekeeping actions have involved several examples of blatant abuses, including harassment, torture, and even murder. UN officials have been involved in drug smuggling, embezzlement, illegal arms trading, and prostitution, all in the name of keeping the peace. In one example, prostitutes were allegedly employed by the UN, and were said to have been transported on UN planes to provide services for UN staff members in hotels paid for by the UN. In other instances, $26.7 million in Rwanda and another $3.9 million in Somalia have vanished mysteriously. The UN investigators dismiss this massive embezzlement as mere mismanagement.[34]

Most recently, an example of UN inaction cost an untold number of lives. A facsimile, dated 11 January 1994, was sent to the UN peacekeeping headquarters in New York. The message warned the UN office of impending genocide in Rwanda. It came from an informant who had specific knowledge of the imminent execution of thousands of Tutsis. No action of any kind was taken to inform, warn, or stop these pending atrocities. Three months later, 800,000 Tutsis were brutally massacred. At the time, the UN peacekeeping office was headed by the current Secretary General of the United Nations, Kofi Annan.[35] The United Nations has proven itself incapable of effectively managing the temporary use of military power. It is clearly imprudent to even consider granting permanent military capacity to such an organization. Nevertheless, the U.S. military has been the target of a long and subtle incremental offensive. The changes have occurred over time and now appear to be entrenched.

The American armed forces seem to be slowly mutating from units designed to protect the welfare of our own nation into groups concerned with safeguarding international interests. With peacekeeping troops stationed in over one hundred nations, Americans should be concerned about how our young men and women in the military are being used and how our tax dollars are being spent. We must support Michael New and others like him so that we can eventually be assured that those admirable individuals who volunteer to protect our nation, are never again told to put on a foreign uniform and take orders from a foreign commander.

The Cold War ended primarily because of President Ronald Reagan's vision, leadership, and skillful command of the armed forces. He created an image of strength and made a proud, powerful military a reality. It can be a reality again, if enough citizens work to reverse the trend and take strong exception to the tactics of those who wish to complete the clandestine disarmament of the armed forces of the United States.

Notes

1. 10 U.S.C. Sec. 502.

2. "Representative James A. Traficant Defends Michael New" (25 January 1996). http://www.reagan.com/HotTopics.main/HotMike/document-1.25.1996.3.html.

3. Richard Carelli, "Soldier Who Refused to Wear UN Patch and Beret Loses Appeal," *Associated Press* (30 March 1998).

4. Michael New is currently appealing his case to the Army Court of Criminal Appeals. The case should be heard sometime in 1998.

5. Al Kamen, "Decisions for the Vice President," *Washington Post* (16 October 1995).

6. See NATO Home Page. http://www.nato.int.

7. The North Atlantic Treaty, http://www.nato.int/docu/basictxt/treaty.htm.

8. Ibid.

9. George Ghetts, Deputy Director of Communications, Libertarian Party press release (8 July 1997). NATO has officially been made an arm of the United Nations in the Peace Agreement in Bosnia.

10. See "Slow down on Expanding NATO," *Tampa Tribune* (11 March 1998).

11. Tom Raum, "Risk Benefits of NATO Expansion," *Associated Press* (1 May 1998).

12. Chemical Weapons Convention can be found at the home page of the U.S. Arms Control and Disarmament Agency. http://www.acda.gov/treaties/cwctext.htm.

13. James M. Inhofe (U.S. Senator R-OK), press release, "Inhofe Opposes Chemical Weapons Treaty" (25 April 1997). See also David A. Keene, "Lott's Chemical Weapons Treaty Vote Gives Conservatives Indigestion," *The Hill* (30 April 1997).

14. United States Constitution, Bill of Rights, Fourth and Fifth Amendments.

15. John Kolbe, "Chemical Weapons Treaty and Invasion," *The Phoenix Gazette* (11 September 1996). See also John Yoo, "The Chemical Weapons Treaty Is Unconstitutional," *Wall Street Journal* (16 April 1997).

16. The Commission on Global Governance, *Our Global Neighborhood: The Report of the Commission on Global Governance* (New York: Oxford University Press, 1995).

17. Ibid., 110.

18. Joseph Farah, "U.S. Secretly Backs Standby UN Army," *WorldNetDaily* (30 April 1998). http://www.worldnetdaily.com/btlines/980430.btl.us.backs.un.army.html.

19. From a speech given by Ingvar Carlsson at Northwestern University in Chicago, Illinois, in the fall of 1997.

20. The Commission on Global Governance, *Our Global Neighborhood: The Report of the Commission on Global Governance,* 111.

21. Ibid., 217.

22. *Canadian North-South Institute's Newsletter,* Vol. 1, No. 1 (1997).

23. State Department Publication 7277.

24. See Duncan L. Clarke, *Politics of Arms Control: The Role and Effectiveness of the U.S. Arms Control and Disarmament Agency* (NY: Free Press, 1979.)

25. Ibid., 31-33.

26. Charter of the United Nations. Concluded at San Francisco, 26 June 1945. Entered into force, 24 October 1945. Reprinted in 1 Weston I.A.1. Article 42.

27. Ibid., Article 43.

28. See Chapter VII of the United Nations Charter.

29. *Clinton Administration Policy on Reforming Multilateral Peace Operations* (P.D.D. 25), U.S. Department of State Publication Number

10161, released by the Bureau of International Organization Affairs (May 1994). This document may be found at George Mason University. http://ralph.gmu.edu/cfpa/peace/pdd25.html.

30. The Combat Arms Survey was sent to Geoff Metcalf by a U.S. Marine. It was accompanied by a written explanation indicating that the survey was conducted at a Marine base in Twentynine Palms, California, on 10 May 1994.

31. Charter of the United Nations. Concluded at San Francisco, 26 June 1945. Entered into force, 24 October 1945. Reprinted in 1 Weston I.A.1. Article 2, Section 4.

32. Ibid., Article 39.

33. Jennifer Gould, *Village Voice* (18 June 1997).

34. Jennifer Gould, "Peacekeepers at Work," *New Republic* (19 June 1997). See also Gould, *Village Voice.*

35. Philip Gourevitch, "Annals of Diplomacy: The Genocide Fax," *The New Yorker* (11 May 1998).

Thirteen

Property Owners:
An Endangered Species

Imagine for a moment the bustling floor of the United States Senate on a typical day in session. A new treaty is under consideration for ratification. The senators and their staff are busily reviewing an eighteen-page document that purports to be the Convention on Biological Diversity,[1] an international United Nations treaty. The treaty is commonly called the Biodiversity Treaty. It was first introduced at the 1992 Earth Summit. The president of the United States already signed the document, and the treaty is being pushed vigorously by the administration and virtually every environmental organization in existence. Meanwhile, a loosely knit and relatively unknown group of citizens are informing the senators that a key component of the treaty is absent from their possession. They warn the Senate not to approve any part of the treaty without first reviewing this crucial missing element. The group speaks of a Global Biodiversity Assessment (GBA),[2] which is said to contain the explicit plans, policies, regulations, and objectives of the treaty. Reportedly, the United Nations, through its organizations, refuses to acknowledge that the GBA even exists.

Providentially, a copy of the GBA is obtained from sources outside the country. It turns out to be a real document, after all, and contains 1,140 frightening pages. When this massive record detailing the specific plans for the future of our country is presented to members of the Senate, Majority Leader George Mitchell removes from the floor the issue of ratification of the treaty.

As unbelievable as it sounds, this is no fictional account. This bizarre congressional saga actually took place in September 1994. Fortunately, opponents of the treaty were alerted to the fact that the UN Environmental Program had been drafting the GBA. They also knew that this more precise and comprehensive document would be incorporated into the Biodiversity Treaty and ultimately used for its implementation. When opponents of the treaty questioned UN groups about the GBA, they simply denied its existence.[3] Apparently, their plan was to eventually submit the language concerning implementation to the U.S. Senate, but only after the treaty was safely ratified. In retrospect, there still is something very peculiar about the progression of events that occurred on that singular day in September. What did this GBA document contain that caused consideration of a major treaty to suddenly be withdrawn from the floor of the Senate? To answer this question, we must examine something called the Wildlands Project.

The Wildlands Project

The Wildlands Project is specifically named and incorporated into the GBA.[4] It is said to be the template for the implementation of the Biodiversity Treaty. The Wildlands Project seeks to radically alter land use of more than fifty percent of the territory of the continental United States, and convert it into a huge wildlife preserve.

The sequestered portions of land would be unimpeded by any commerce, industry, or private property ownership. Severely restricting the use of sizable parcels of land in the United States is the brainchild of some of the proponents of the most caustic type of environmental activism, such as the founder of Earth First, David Foreman, and deep ecologist Reed Noss. The Wildlands Project is the result of a collaboration between the United Nations Environmental Program and extreme environmental NGOs, with creative direction furnished by Foreman and Noss. In preparing the language for the Biodiversity Treaty, the United Nations sought the services of several international environmental organizations, including the International Union for Conservation of Nature, the Worldwide Fund for Nature, and the World Resources Institute. All organizations conferring had one significant trait in common; they believed it was necessary to set aside massive portions of land as reserves and corridors in order to protect biodiversity. Biodiversity is a term that is used quite frequently in UN documents. It has no clear definition, but is utilized to signify a broad concept that encompasses every aspect of ecological relationships between living things. The Wildlands

Project[5] is a master plan that creates a grid of wilderness areas across the nation. Consistent with its deep ecology philosophy, it seeks to have wildlife and wilderness restored to a pre-industrial state.

The first step in implementing the GBA program and Wildlands Project is to identify existing protected lands such as federal and state wilderness areas, parks, and refuges. These territories would then be designated as initial core reserves and would be zoned exclusively for non-human use. Core reserves are pure wilderness areas created to preserve biodiversity. All species are allowed free access to core reserves, except for one: *Homo sapiens*. Once core reserves have been established and human beings have been banished, the regions must be completely protected. This is done, according to the Wildlands section of the GBA, by establishing a protective segment surrounding the core reserve area. This protective segment is referred to as a buffer zone. Very limited, non-commercial use by human beings will be permitted within buffer zones. These restrictions are harmonious with the philosophy that the needs of non-humans must take precedence over the needs of people. Naturally, vehicles would be denied access to any part of a buffer zone. Buffer zones enable the land that is impacted by the treaty to be expanded exponentially. However, the taking of land would not stop there. The long-range plan involves the eventual confiscation of hundreds of millions of acres of private land, in addition to the public appropriations.

The next step involved in implementing the Wildlands Project is the creation of corridors. Corridors are tracts of land that connect core reserves to one another. In order to preserve species, other than Homo sapiens, in core reserves, equal pathways upon which wildlife can freely travel in and out of the core wilderness areas must be established. Large masses of territory that contain core reserves and buffer zones must be connected with specific strips of land so that the various forms of wildlife can move unrestrained and without human interference. These strips of land constitute a kind of eco-freeway system. Anyone who has the misfortune to own property in or close to one of the core reserves, buffer zones, or corridors will be forced to have the rights of the property in question transferred to public agencies or private environmental organizations.

The core reserve and the surrounding buffer zone together are referred to as a biosphere reserve. The United Nations World Heritage and Biosphere Programs currently designate forty-seven biosphere reserves. The regions include large areas of California, Washington, Arizona, New Mexico, Nevada, and other states. This is where local government bureaucracies, in conjunction with NGOs, will be able to limit the use of land at will, with the preservation of biodiversity in mind.

Finally, once biosphere reserves have been established and human activity in these regions is intensely restricted, a zone of cooperation is set up. Zones of cooperation are areas that extend around biosphere reserves. A property owner who happens to own acreage in one of these impacted areas could find the land taken away, or its use severely restricted, without the appropriate compensation required by the Fifth Amendment of the Constitution. Section 10.5 of the GBA[6] speaks specifically of the need to relocate citizens outside of corridors and core reserves. According to the Global Biodiversity Assessment, this relocation would take place over a twenty-to-fifty-year period. Since the requirements of non-humans take priority over those of human beings in core reserves, buffer zones, and corridors, this plan, if effectuated, is a dream come true for deep ecologists. For the rest of us, it amounts to the sheer destruction of what we consider to be, and generally admire as, modern civilization.

A drastic reduction in human activity all over the country would be required for the GBA program to be implemented. Approximately one-fourth of the land in the continental United States would be returned to wilderness status, and an even greater percentage would have very limited human use. Rather than matters of usage being handled by the corresponding states where the land is located, the GBA fundamentally changes the traditional land use control equations. It sets up new bureaucracies called Bioregional Commissions. These commissions would be administered by the government, in partnership with NGOs.

The NGOs fall far short of representing average citizens, and their regulatory schemes offer no way for property owners to actively participate in the process. When citizens are forced to relocate to only those areas that are approved for human activity, then industry, farming, forestry, mining, and other commercial enterprises will either be shut down or forced to move. This will result in economic dislocation, unemployment, and a lower standard of living for all the people of our nation. The average person shudders at such a proposal for the future, but the organizers of the Biodiversity Treaty do not view these effects as negative. From their perspective, the standard of living and consumption habits of typical American citizens are recklessly excessive and contribute significantly to ecological problems around the world.

Section 9 of the GBA[7] refers to the habits of the American consumer. It concludes that our consumption habits are unsustainable. However, it does propose a solution. Consumers can make a Hobson's choice of either drastically reducing global population, lowering it to less than half the people currently occupying the world, or returning all populations to a primitive, agrarian lifestyle. This is not a choice that most Americans would regard as consistent with our guaranteed liberties.

By using core reserves, buffer zones, corridors, biospheres, and zones of cooperation, as planned in the Wildlands Project, Section 10 of the GBA, the World Heritage Convention, and the Man and Biosphere Program, the majority of the United States could eventually be controlled by an international bureaucracy that uses environmentalism as a pretext for maintaining a virtual stranglehold on the nation.

Confiscation without Representation

It is difficult to believe that a world treaty, such as the United Nations Convention on Biodiversity, would suggest such a nightmarish plan. It is equally difficult to understand how a president could sign such a treaty. Yet President Bill Clinton did exactly that in 1993. To exacerbate matters, the Clinton administration made it clear that convincing the U.S. Senate to ratify the Biodiversity Treaty was a prime objective. Typical of their furtive strategies, the rejection of the treaty by the Senate, pursuant to its constitutional approval power, did not prevent the administration from implementing provisions in incremental steps through executive orders and memoranda.

A good example of the administration's use of circumvention is found when we examine the Man and Biosphere Program.[8] The United Nations created the program in 1971. It is an international initiative designed to assist the implementation of many aspects of the Biodiversity Treaty. In order to support this pro-

gram, in January 1996 President Clinton issued Executive Order
12986,[9] which extended immunity from lawsuit to the International Union for Conservation of Nature and Natural Resources
(IUCNNR). This organization was then granted a privilege that
is normally given only to foreign diplomats. Why would the
president offer such extraordinary treatment to one particular
organization? It is because the group is a key vehicle in creating
and promoting the Man and Biosphere Program. This program
has been implemented by the State Department, again bypassing
congressional action, using various memoranda.[10] The program
has been operating covertly, utilizing UN organizations and
NGOs, with very little input from local citizens.

The Man and Biosphere Program is busy designating core
areas and laying the groundwork for the realization of the goals
set forth in the Wildlands Project and the Biodiversity Treaty. Its
stated purpose is to find solutions for environmental problems.
However, a veiled plan to transfer sovereignty from U.S. territory
to the United Nations is evident in the program. Quietly and
almost unnoticed, the administration has placed forty-seven large
areas of land under the UN banner. These biosphere reserves
constitute a land mass greater than the state of Wyoming.[11]

The principles of the GBA have become the tacit policy
guidelines for the Department of Interior and the Environmental
Protection Agency. The tenets of the GBA and the Wildlands
Project have also been embraced by highly influential environmental organizations such as the Sierra Club and the Nature
Conservancy. Using the GBA as a beacon, environmentalists at
all levels of government are attempting to fulfill its highly intem-
perate objectives. To advance these goals, the United States is
being divided into twenty-one bioregions, and the current federal
policy is to eventually eradicate county and state boundaries and
replace them with bioregional borders. International treaties are
not only being employed to restrict the use of and access to these
selected areas, but they are also being utilized to impact privately-
owned land located outside these sites.

Documents of UNESCO describe the Man and Biosphere
Program as the first step in implementing the Convention on
Biological Diversity. In a similar bureaucratic control structure to
the GBA, the Man and Biosphere Program is governed by
unelected, unaccountable commissions that consist of selected

public and private organizations. Of course, the usual environmental NGOs figure prominently in the design. If things proceed as intended, the owners of real property, to their dismay, are
going to find that their rights have been modified by new land
use regulations, and they will have had no representative voice in
the proceedings.

Up the River

The most recent assault on private property rights and state
sovereignty, courtesy of the Clinton administration, is the American Heritage Rivers Initiative (AHRI).[12] This initiative was in-
stigated by the White House in a swift and quiet manner and was
executed without congressional approval. Its purpose is ostensibly
to provide federal assistance to local communities in order to
protect the environment, preserve waterfronts, and conserve local
history. Like so many other innocent-sounding proposals, it seeks
to accomplish something much more grave and perilous to our
individual freedoms. The initiative is merely the repackaging of
the Heritage Areas Act, which Congress failed to pass in 1996.
Essentially, the Heritage Areas Act would have been the same as
AHRI, with the exception that Congress would have had the
authority to designate areas as "heritage zones." Congress's rejection of the initiative meant very little to the Clinton administration. The administration simply acted as a legislature, ignoring
the Constitution. On 11 September 1997 President Clinton issued Executive Order 13061, making the American Heritage
Rivers Initiative official. The waters within the border of a state
have been, up to the present time, the exclusive province of state
sovereignty. What the executive order for the AHRI does represents an unconstitutional transfer of power from the states to the
federal government.[13]

The AHRI is an effort to create federal control over large
parcels of land adjacent to U.S. rivers. The program began with
ten rivers, but fourteen more were added in July 1998, and, in
due time, well over one hundred rivers will be included. The
private property rights of owners of real estate along the banks of
the rivers will be severely impacted and hundreds of thousands of
acres of land will ultimately be affected. Regulations for each
river system are governed by a presidentially-appointed bureau-
crat, while the President's Council on Environmental Quality

administers the entire plan. Each year, additional rivers will be selected for inclusion by the president.

Down the Shaft

In another incredible assault on the sovereignty of a state over land within its jurisdiction, nearly two million acres in the state of Utah were instantly transformed into a national monument. This gigantic transfer of land was not the result of representative government. It was not accomplished by an act of the Utah legislature, or an effort of the U.S. Congress. It was the result of an executive order. In dictatorial fashion, it required no debate, no vote, no lobbying. With just one signature, the land was vaporized out of the hands of Utah's citizens. The American public was led to believe that the land was a giant wilderness park, government owned anyway. However, this is not the case. The land that was seized included hundreds of thousands of acres of private land as well. The people of Utah not only lost control, they lost money too. Tens of billions of tons of high quality coal, trillions of cubic feet of natural gas, three million tons of zirconium and titanium, and billions of barrels of oil are said to be situated beneath the Utah land. If the estimates are correct, this land constitutes one of the greatest untapped natural resources in the entire United States.

Utahans were in no way consulted prior to the decision being made. The state government was not provided with advanced notice, nor was it given the opportunity to be heard prior to the confiscation. In fact, the state of Utah discovered the loss of this incredible resource on the very morning that the president announced the news.

The World Heritage Treaty

The World Heritage Convention of 1972[14] granted a new and dangerous authority to UNESCO. This group was given the power to designate certain historical, cultural, and wholly revered locations, within the United States, as world heritage sites. The World Heritage Committee was set up, pursuant to the World Heritage Convention, in order to establish procedures, financing, and regulations for cultural and national heritage sites throughout the world. The idea of preserving our common heritage may sound rather noble. However, when a UN plaque is observed on

the Statue of Liberty, indicating that it is under the umbrella of
the United Nations, as can be witnessed right now, such fond
feelings for the whole notion of collective protection quickly dis-
sipate. Additional UN plaques can be seen posted at Independence Hall, the Grand Canyon, Carlsbad Caverns, Yellowstone
National Park, and many other sites that are held in such high
esteem by Americans. The rationale for this takeover is that certain sites have such unusual value that their protection is the
responsibility of all humanity.

The United Nations is earmarking numerous land masses
around the world for classification as heritage sites. For example,
in Australia, land so designated was rendered in violation of the
property rights of local ranchers and farmers. In New Zealand,
almost fifty percent of South Island has been assigned to receive
"heritage site" treatment. In the United States, Yellowstone
National Park has gained some special attention as a world heritage site. Yellowstone National Park consists of over 2.2 million
acres of land. As a world heritage site, it is effectively under the
jurisdiction of the United Nations. With the environmental perspective of those who control the UN, Yellowstone National
Park will eventually have a substantial buffer zone around it,
which could include parts of Utah, Idaho, Wyoming, and Mon-
tana. Over 15 million acres of American soil could someday be
affected.

In 1995 the Crown Butte New World Gold Mine, located
five miles outside Yellowstone, was shut down, not because of
any regulation passed by the U.S. government or the state of
Wyoming, but because it happened to be located too close to
Yellowstone National Park. According to the United Nations,
the mine fell within the buffer zone. Even though no environmental problems had been reported to the state agencies,
UNESCO officials sought the mine's closure. This was done to
establish jurisdiction over the buffer zone. Wrapping itself in the
cloak of environmental preservation, the Clinton administration
allied itself with the United Nations in opposition to the gold
mine. This is a clear case where international law was used to
defeat both federal and state sovereignty. Moreover, it was a
blatant attack on the sum and substance of private property ownership.

UNESCO has already asserted a claim on twenty world

heritage sites in the United States. Included are the following national parks: Olympic, Redwood, Yosemite, Yellowstone, Grand Canyon, Mammoth Cave, Mesa Verde, Great Smokey Mountains, Everglades, Hawaii Volcanoes, Carlsbad Caverns, and Glacier. Also claimed are such historical and cultural icons as the Statue of Liberty, Independence Hall, and Monticello. The change in the character and administration of these sites has been conducted covertly without input from members of the local communities. UNESCO decides which sites to choose for distinguished treatment by having selected federal and state officials work together with NGOs. Paragraph 14 of the *Operational Guidelines of the World Heritage Convention* discusses this covert implementation in typical international law language:

> To avoid possible embarrassment to those concerns, state parties (to the convention) should refrain from giving undo publicity to the fact that a property has been nominated for inscription pending the final decision of the committee on the nomination in question.[15]

Much like the philosophy of the Wildlands Project and the Biodiversity Treaty, buffer zones and corridors are part of the thinking process in the selection of world heritage sites. When Yellowstone National Park was declared a world heritage site, the federal government, through UNESCO, expanded the core area to include a buffer zone. In this way, the gold mine, which was a considerable distance from the actual location of Yellowstone National Park, could be affected. The core reserve and buffer zone were referred to as the "greater Yellowstone ecosystem." This expanded the roughly 2 million acres within the park, to allow the annexation of another 15 to 20 million acres located on the outside of the core reserve.

Once a heritage site has been designated, international environmentalists join forces with domestic environmentalists to attack the rights of landowners surrounding it. For example, when Everglades National Park was recognized as a heritage site in 1993, farmers located north of the park were inundated with a host of new restrictions, regulations, and land use laws that have severely impacted the agricultural industry in the area. In an apparent imitation of the Biodiversity Treaty, the World Heritage Program has specific language in Paragraphs 17 and 44 of its operating guidelines describing buffer zones that are free from human encroachment. The World Heritage Convention is a key component that, together with the Biodiversity Treaty and the Man and Biosphere Program, is designed to appropriate an extraordinary portion of American property rights in a quiet, steady manner, without the normal obstacles of due process getting in the way.

The Trend is No Friend

These kinds of comprehensive and surreptitious plans appear to be veiled attempts to transfer sovereignty from United States territory to the United Nations. A total of sixty-seven United States parcels, national parks, or historical landmarks have now been placed under the effective control and sovereignty of the United Nations.[16] The transfer of these sites could not have occurred without the cooperation of the United States government. The problem is that the conveyance is happening without the American public being informed. A certain amount of sovereignty has already been yielded by virtue of the United States being party to the World Heritage Treaty. Our remaining sovereignty could be completely surrendered if the United States ever becomes an official and completely active participant of the Biodiversity Treaty. International lawyers may differ as to the legal effects of these treaties, with respect to individual freedoms, but it is clear by the way provisions have already been implemented, that the net effect is to override individual rights and diminish both federal and state sovereignty.

The sovereignty being relinquished by the United States is happening in an indirect and circuitous way. Defenders of these programs will point to language in UN documents, which states that the sovereignty of the United States is to remain unaffected. However, as is true of many of the internationally-designed regulatory schemes, such language is not very comforting. The treaties bind participating countries to only those uses that are specifically prescribed for the lands in question. Our sovereignty is to be subservient to the designated uses, notwithstanding any generalized language included to create a false sense of security.

When environmentalists describe the concept of biodiversity, it can sound incredibly appealing. The U.S. Senate certainly thought so, until they saw the entire text of the treaty they were about to approve in September of 1994. We must be diligent in scrutinizing these international regulatory programs. Most Americans support preserving our national parks and wildlife. Yet when admirable objects are employed to obscure activities and deprive citizens of constitutional protections, the curtains must be parted so that the truth may clearly be seen.

Notes

1. The Convention on Biological Diversity. Concluded at Rio de Janeiro, 6 June 1992. Entered into force, 29 December 1993. Reprinted in 5A Weston V.H.22.

2. V.H. Heywood, ed., *Global Biodiversity Assessment* (New York: Cambridge University Press, 1996).

3. *Biodiversity-The Key to Destroying Property Rights and the U.S. Constitution,* videorecording of television broadcast of "The Truth As I See It" on 14 October 1995. (Bangor, Maine: Environmental Perspectives, Inc., 1995).

4. Heywood, Global Biodiversity Assessment, Section 10.4.2.2.3.

5. Wildlands Project Home Page. http://www.wildlandsproject.org.

6. Heywood, Global Biodiversity Assessment, Section 10.5.

7. Ibid., Section 9.

8. UNESCO Man and Biosphere Program Home Page. http://www.unesco.org/mab/themabnet.htm.

9. *The Federal Register,* 61 FR 1693; 22 January 1996.

10. U.S. Man and Biosphere Program Home Page. http://www.mabnetamericas.org/home2.html.

11. Natural Resources Defense Council, *What is a Biosphere Reserve?* http://mail.igc.apc.org/nrdc/bkgrd/fobio.html.

12. American Heritage Rivers Initiative. http://www.amrivers.org.

13. "Federal River Grab Coming Next Week: 'Heritage' Initiative to Give U.S. More Land Control," *WorldNetDaily* (21 January 1998). http//www.worldnetdaily.com. See also Phyllis Schlafly, "Clinton Is Selling Us down the Rivers," (4 March 1998). http://www.eagle forum.org/column/1998/mar98/98-03-04.html. (President Clinton amended Executive Orders 13061 and 13080 to include up to 20 rivers on 27 July 1998, *U.S. Newswire* 202-347-2270.)

14. World Heritage Convention of 1972. Ratified by the United States on 12 July 1973. Gopher: gopher://gopher.unesco.org:70/11/gopher.

15. Ibid.

16. Testimony of Representative Helen Chenoweth (R-ID) before the House Committee on Resources (10 June 1997).

Fourteen

Courting a Global Judiciary

In 1947 the United Nations asked the International Law Commission to draft a statute in an effort to institute a permanent criminal court. Many people scoffed at such an idea as mere fantasy. Others warned that the establishment of a world criminal court was imminent and would lead to judicial tyranny. Today the idea is very close to becoming a reality. The strategy for implementation is to establish an International Criminal Court (ICC) through use of a multilateral treaty.[1] In this way, the plan will bind every participating member country. Unlike the World Court, that acts as an international civil court where nations can bring complaints against other nations, a permanent world criminal court will have as part of its design some sort of presiding prosecutor. The organizers of this court contemplate that the prosecutor will have broad authority to initiate an investigation and carry it through to adjudication. Since this court will be criminal rather than civil in nature, these investigations will be conducted against private individuals or corporations, as opposed to nations.

Presumption of Ignorance

Since any prosecution by the ICC would lead to a criminal trial, at this point it remains highly uncertain what protections would be afforded the accused. Attorneys and judges involved in the proceedings would come from different legal systems around the globe. Legal traditions in many other countries do not hold the notions of presumption of innocence, right of the accused to confront witnesses, and many of the other constitutional protections mandated by the American system of government.

A permanent criminal court will have jurisdiction over genocide, war crimes, crimes against humanity, aggression, and other crimes established through treaties adopted by the United Nations. It is the *other crimes established by treaties* language that is most troubling.[2] These words could be used to justify the prosecution of an individual who failed to carry out a provision of a particular treaty. For example, if an individual breached a portion of one of the treaties that deals with social behavior, such as the Convention on the Rights of the Child or the Convention on the Elimination of All Forms of Discrimination against Women, that person could be prosecuted in an International Criminal Court. As another illustration, the ICC could prosecute an individual or corporate violator of an environmental treaty, such as the Convention on Biological Diversity or the World Heritage Convention. Needless to say, the repercussions from the installation of a court system of this type would be enormous.

Despite the seriousness of this unprecedented agenda in international law, most people are unaware, or they may not fully comprehend, the magnitude of the issue, especially when it comes to measuring the possible effects that a court of this kind could have on the personal lives of citizens. The subject of foreign affairs lulls many people to sleep, and there is a belief that a permanent criminal court is just too remote a concept to warrant public concern. Yet there are some glaring examples of how established international tribunals, such as the one described, could interfere within the jurisdiction of an entire nation.

Not O.K. for U.K.

A British boy whose stepfather used corporal punishment to correct him appealed to the European Commission on Human Rights. The boy argued that Britain had failed to protect his right to freedom from degrading punishment. He asserted that this right was guaranteed by the European Convention on Human Rights, a treaty that Britain signed. The Commission ruled in favor of the boy, and the case will now be heard by the European Court of Human Rights. Britain may find itself ordered to pass new legislation that abolishes corporal punishment. Furthermore, if this transpires, international lawyers will cite the case as a precedent against corporal punishment, forcing all other countries that happen to be a party to the treaty to enact similar legislation. This is a preview of what can occur when international judicial power is allowed to proceed unchecked.

Some of the drafters of the ICC documentation have proposed a safeguard that would allow the Security Council to veto a given prosecution, but this does not provide sufficient shelter. A citizen should not have to rely on the government of the United States to exercise a veto in order to obtain protection from criminal prosecution by an international court. After all, foreign relations, politics, or even world trade, could easily influence such a decision. Instead, individual nations should enforce their existing war crime legislation, as they are obliged to do under the Hague Convention of 1907[3] and the Geneva Convention of 1949.[4] If an unusual case requiring special treatment should arise, a temporary tribunal could be set up, as has occurred in the past, with proven effectiveness.

Global Judicial Institutions

Since the end of the Cold War, new judicial institutions have emerged from nearly every corner of the international legal landscape. In addition to temporary tribunals that have dealt with criminal law, judicial regimes have been developed for trade law, human rights, the law of the sea, commercial law, public international law, and environmental law. This is a foreshadowing of what could aptly be called the coming international legal order.

The International Court of Justice (ICJ)[5] is based in the Netherlands at the Hague. The ICJ is currently the principal judicial organ of the United Nations. It functions as an international civil justice institution established for the purpose of resolving disputes between nations. It is also commonly referred to as the World Court. Since it was created in April 1946, it has heard over seventy cases and issued twenty advisory opinions for various international organizations. The ICJ jurisdiction is based on consent. Nations in dispute bind themselves by signing a treaty or making a declaration accepting the compulsory jurisdiction of the court. The United States was one of the founding members of the ICJ. Ironically, the U.S. was compelled to withdraw its acceptance of the ICJ's compulsory jurisdiction in 1986 because the court had assumed jurisdiction over a lawsuit brought by Nicaragua against the United States. The lawsuit was a highly political action by a country that despised the American lifestyle and economic system. In a similar political use of the court in

1997, Libya attempted to use its jurisdiction to avoid the surrender of suspects in the 1988 jet bombing that killed 270 people. Presently, the UN Charter allows the Security Council to enforce judgments of the ICJ.[6] Of course, the power of the ICJ could be expanded tremendously if the UN had the military and financial resources to compel compliance.[7] This seems to provide one more reason why the expressed desire of the international legal community for UN military capabilities and global taxes could have serious consequences.

The newly formed International Tribunal for the Law of the Sea (ITLOS) was established to interpret the United Nations Convention on the Law of the Sea. Countries that are party to the Law of the Sea Treaty are required to submit any dispute over interpretation to ITLOS. Nations can opt to go to the ICJ or choose binding arbitration, unless the dispute is over seabed mining.

The World Trade Organization (WTO), based in Geneva, came into existence on 1 January 1995. It acts as an international court for trade dispute resolution. Disputes submitted to the WTO are given to panels assembled by a division of the WTO called the Dispute Settlement Body (DSB). If a dispute remains unresolved, or a party is dissatisfied with a result, an appeal is made to a standing appellate body established by the DSB.[8] As discussed in Chapter Eleven, the appellate body issued a major decision against the United States in 1996. This decision involved the sale of foreign gasoline that the U.S. considered to be below EPA standards. The gasoline deemed substandard was being exported by Venezuela and Brazil. The appellate body held that the EPA rules in the United States that applied to gasoline imports discriminated against foreign oil producers.

There are numerous affiliated international courts and tribunals, and the reason for their existence is fairly simple. There is an increased willingness on the part of many nations to allow certain specialized areas of their sovereignty to be transferred to these internationally constituted courts. Since examples of international judicial organizations have multiplied in an attempt to address every conceivable area of the law at the international level, it was only a matter of time before a cry for the establishment of a permanent court for international adjudication of criminal cases would resonate in the world community.

Crime, Punishment, and Sovereignty

Historically, the prosecution of crimes and the subsequent punishment for offenses have been the sole prerogative of individual nations. The right to penalize strikes at the heart of the sovereignty issue. Despite this reality, governments have been meeting in formal sessions at the UN headquarters in New York for years, trying to decide how to structure the world's first permanent criminal court, the International Criminal Court (ICC).

A conference was held in July of 1998 to finalize and to adopt a multilateral International Criminal Court Treaty. The Clinton administration continued to fully support the plan, even after suffering a diplomatic defeat when the majority of the world's nations approved the treaty over the objections of the United States. When completely implemented, the court will have jurisdiction over genocide, war crimes, and crimes against humanity. These crimes have traditionally been associated with international law and with temporary tribunals that were set up historically. However, the crimes of terrorism, drug trafficking, aggression, and selected noncompliance with treaty provisions have now been added to the list. When the ICC takes full effect, it will not be long before a call will go out for a police force or an enforcement mechanism for the court. This, of course, could be handled by a permanent United Nations military force that has been proposed so often.

A series of meetings of international lawyers intent on creating this permanent criminal tribunal led to the adoption of the treaty in Rome. The Preparatory Committee on the Establishment of an International Criminal Court held its third and fourth sessions in February and August of 1997, respectively. Each of these meetings brought the world one step closer to the establishment of a permanent criminal court. The 1994 draft statute drawn up by the International Law Commission consisted of more than 300 pages of proposed amendments. It became known as the *telephone book* because of its length.[9]

The initial issue that the group debated involved the definition of crime. The first crime discussed was genocide. Some fundamental questions were left unanswered concerning whether to include so-called ancillary crimes. These ancillary crimes include conspiracy to commit genocide, direct and public incitement to commit genocide, attempt to commit genocide, and complicity in genocide. The vagueness and ambiguity inherent in these ancillary crimes leave an opening for potential prosecutorial abuse. The issues of whether a prosecution can be vetoed by the Security Council, and how many votes it would take for such a veto, were hotly contested matters, as was the independence of the prosecutor to initiate an investigation and present an indictment on his or her own.[10]

These issues were resolved against the interests of the United States by the Rome assembly when the group categorically rejected any veto rights or oversight of ICC decisions. The ICC judges and their staff of investigators will be free to prosecute Americans in the armed forces. The treaty will involve eighteen judges from different nation-states, elected at the United Nations by secret ballot, involving only those countries that will be party to the treaty, even though the treaty binds non-participant countries.[11]

The intent of the people who worked to create an ICC is clear from the language expressed in a report on the Preparatory Committee's progress. "It was generally agreed that an ICC would have jurisdictions only where national courts were unable or unwilling to deal with the crime in a fair way."[12] This means that the court would have the power to superimpose jurisdiction on U.S. courts. Those who are promoting the court envision that there will be cases where an ICC will assume priority, thus encroaching on both the jurisdiction and the sovereignty of the judicial system of the United States.

The temporary tribunals that have historically handled the concerns of war crimes, such as genocide and crimes against humanity, were limited in both time and scope. The UN plan for an ICC not only creates a permanent tribunal, but also expands the crimes to include those involving aggression and crimes established pursuant to specified treaties. The whole idea of a global prosecutor enforcing provisions of treaties against individuals clashes with the spirit of American values.

Is This Court Necessary?

Proponents of a permanent criminal court are quick to point out that temporary tribunals, such as those set up for war crimes in the former Yugoslavia and in Rwanda, are not as efficient as the ICC will be. However, there are a multitude of problems associated with such a court. For example, how will the prosecutors be chosen? No doubt there are certain members of the international community who would have wanted to prosecute General Norman Schwarzkopf for his leadership role in the successful bombing campaigns of the Persian Gulf War. It is quite possible, in a UN-controlled courtroom, that the prosecutor could be a colleague of Saddam Hussein. Issues involved in a situation of the type described must be carefully considered before the United States gives its stamp of approval to the ICC.

The establishment of the ICC is of great concern to the Defense Department, which has American military personnel deployed around the world to deal with many of the same issues that such a court will consider. Pentagon chiefs are painfully aware of events surrounding the Vietnam War in the 1960s and 1970s, and the military operation in Central America in the 1980s. The prosecution of American officials and members of the armed forces as war criminals was aggressively pursued by those opposed to these combat actions.

Americans admit that their legal system is flawed in some ways, but it is certainly not as imperfect as many of the other legal systems around the world. Basically, there is no other legal system where individual rights and due process are as respected as in the law of the United States. An ICC, however, would subject citizens of the United States to different, and most likely inferior, laws.

Still, the U.S. may have sent the wrong signals in negotiations that led to the establishment of the ICC. Chief U.S. negotiator David J. Scheffer, the State Department's ambassador-at-large for war crimes issues, used deliberate, noncommittal language at a breakfast discussion sponsored by the Twentieth Century Fund. This was construed by many as an indication of compromise on the part of the U.S. on key issues that were in play during the 1998 July conference in Rome. Perhaps this is one of the reasons the ICC treaty adopted in Rome gives virtually unlimited jurisdiction to the global criminal court and creates a prosecutor with the power to initiate investigations and prosecute individuals from countries that are not a party to the treaty.[13]

Unfortunately, it is the nature and character of the leadership of the UN not only to seek further expansion of the powers of a permanent ICC, but also to administer its proceedings in an inequitable and biased manner. The UN has a pattern of selectively ignoring the facts when Communist nations engage in war crimes. The creation of such a global judiciary, with foreign judges presiding, vested with the power to conduct trials of American citizens for potentially ill-defined crimes, is a formula for legal chicanery.

One thing is clear: American citizens must be alerted to the plans for the ICC. Armed with pertinent information, our populace must make sure that representatives are elected at all levels of government who will resist any attempt to place a global prosecutor in this untenable position of authority. The issue must be diligently followed and opposition must be ever present, so that this judicial monster is never granted the power to wield influence over the personal lives of U.S. citizens.

Notes

1. NGO Coalition for an International Criminal Court. http:// www.igc.org/icc.

2. Tony Freemantle, "Creation of World Tribunal Moves Ever Closer to Reality," *Houston Chronicle* (15 November 1996).

3. The Hague Convention of 1907, Pamphlet Series of the Carnegie Endowment for International Peace. Division of International Law, 16 Volumes (Washington, DC: The Endowment, 1915).

4. The Geneva Convention of 1949, protocols of the Geneva Conventions of 12 August 1949 (Washington, DC: Dept. of Defense, Dept. of Army, Headquarters. 1979).

5. Statute of the International Court of Justice. Concluded at San Francisco, 26 June 1945. Entered into force, 24 October 1945. Reprinted in 1 Weston I.H.2.

6. Ibid., Article 41; Charter of the United Nations. Concluded at San Francisco, 26 June 1945. Entered into force, 24 October 1945. Reprinted in 1 Weston I.A.1, Article 37.

7. See Gerald S. Schatz, "Keith Highet on the World Court," *American Society of International Law Newsletter 1*, 8 (May/June 1997).

8. Understanding on Rules and Procedures Governing the Settlement of Disputes. Entered into force, 1 January 1995. Reprinted in 4 Weston IV.C.3.

9. Christopher Keith Hall, "The First Two Sessions of the UN Preparatory Committee on the Establishment of an International Criminal Court," *American Journal of International Law* (January 1997): 177.

10. Christopher Keith Hall, "The Third and Fourth Session of the UN Preparatory Committee on the Establishment of an International Criminal Court," *American Journal of International Law* (January 1998): 124.

11. See Thomas W. Lippman, "War Crimes Court Approval Gives U.S. a Dilemma," *Washington Post* (23 July 1998). *American Society of International Law Newsletter* (January/February 1998), 9.

12. Ibid.

13. David Frum, "The International Criminal Court Must Die," *The Weekly Standard* (10 August 1998), 27. John M. Goshko, "A Shift on Role of UN Court? Envoy Suggests U.S. May Alter Demands on Proposed Tribunal," *Washington Post* (18 March 1998).

Fifteen

Prophecy and Patriotism

Two thousand years ago, on the island of Patmos, an aging seer transcribed divinely inspired prophetic and apocalyptic visions. These vivid descriptions have been preserved and passed down as the sacred scriptural writings known as the Book of Revelation. Many of the predictions set forth in the Scripture are apparent all around us. The trend toward world governance, the rejection of religious faith, the embrace of neo-pagan beliefs, and the gradual emergence of a global economy are all consistent with the biblical prophecy expressed by this New Testament oracle. The Scripture predicts a one-world economy, government, and religion.[1] The European Union, which could very well be the revised Roman Empire, predicted in Daniel and Revelation, has now officially established a common currency. Great Britain was originally opposed to the European Union, but the present government played an integral role in negotiating and finalizing the details for the common monetary system. Ironically, the official poster for the United States of Europe portrays the federation of nations as the biblical Tower of Babel.

These are all signs that should be observed and analyzed in a thoughtful manner. Yet, despite the prophetic revelations, we have some very important obligations to which we must attend in the process of living our lives in a righteous manner.

First of all, we are to be good stewards of the bounty that has been so generously bestowed upon us. In America, citizenship is undoubtedly one of our greatest blessings. The precious privileges we enjoy are often taken for granted, but these rights were ardently defended and carefully shaped by spiritually minded individuals who sought the guidance of our Creator from the very inception of our nation. Our founding documents, the Declaration of Independence and the Constitution, demonstrate unprecedented inspiration that was providentially directed. The way our government has been formulated, we have neither monarchs nor kings, but, instead, our political leaders are our employees. We have a moral duty to maintain and preserve the freedoms that our fore-fathers prayerfully charted. We must not allow ambivalence, leth-argy, or piety to hinder us from engaging in the vital duty of patriotic custodianship.

Second, we must remain eternally optimistic. The faithful have sometimes been confused by the teaching to be *in* the world but not *of* the world. Christ's words may even seem a bit abstract to some when he states that his Kingdom is not of this world.[2] Some people have interpreted this to mean that the Kingdom must be outside of the existing world, or a dominion that is to come in the future, rather than one that exists now. However, sometimes engaging in a focus on the future takes its form as an obsession with various end times scenarios. Certain believers may acquire an outlook of futility about their lives on earth. To sug-gest that the spiritual is totally absent from the world, until the coming of a future event, can create a real separation between faith and culture. The loser in such an equation is society as a whole. The lack of contribution from those who are morally minded results in a cultural decline by default, as the population suffers from the lack of ethical input.

On the other hand, when spiritual actuality is viewed as inseparable from the world, it acknowledges the wholeness and integrity of creation. We recognize that all of the elements that comprise our humanity, including the social and cultural compo-nents, fall within the sovereignty of the Almighty. With this hallowed perspective, we can fulfill our responsibilities and per-mit ourselves to be instruments in effecting positive change.

Third, we must be wise and skillful in our approach. Respon-sible citizenship takes courage. Cynicism and disillusionment are dangerous and contagious maladies that induce otherwise virtu-ous people to retreat from their civic and moral obligations. We have observed how the enemies of freedom operate at the inter-national level. They mount attacks on the sanctity of life, the traditional family, educational institutions, religious expression, and individual ownership of private property. They form coali-tions to accomplish their goals and are satisfied to work for long periods of time to achieve incremental progress. We have seen organizations, such as the American Civil Liberties Union, con-tinually and steadfastly strive to remove any semblance of public religious expression from our schools and common areas.

Yet those who understand the original intent of the founding fathers also realize the true source of our freedoms. The freedoms to be born, to live, to raise and educate our children, to worship, and to own private property are sacred rights. Aleksandr Solzhenitsyn, who stared into the face of totalitarianism in the Soviet Union, spoke of the loss of freedoms in the Western world when he said, "Tragically, however, the free west will only believe it when it is no longer free. To quote a Russian proverb, 'When it happens you will know it is true, but then it is too late.' "[3]

There is a battle taking place between good and evil. For good to triumph, the adversary must be fully examined and confronted. Our battlefields lie within societal institutions, cultural mores, and political operations. We must employ intelligent strategies, as well as prudent restraint when necessary, in our efforts.[4]

Fourth, we must be the salt and light.[5] To obey this mandate, responsible citizens must write, speak, defend, protest, legislate, and otherwise engage the culture. When we withdraw into a protected cocoon, we concede the rudder of society to the moral relativists. As C.S. Lewis so aptly said, "We cannot remain silent and concede everything away."[6] As citizens, we must be obedient to our government, as established by the Creator.[7] Still, patriotism involves more than mere obedience. Without fully partaking in our governmental processes, the rare and costly liberties that enable Americans to pursue meaningful lives are jeopardized. Freedom is not self-sustaining. Rather, it is something that must be forever cultivated and safeguarded. The electorate cannot maintain fundamental freedoms without engaging in the political process. In order to be properly represented, individuals must fully participate. At the very least, this means being informed. It also means casting votes in an election. When necessary, it means bravely taking a public stand to defend and protect our rights.

In addition, we must also try to recover ground that has been lost. Many now say that our culture has moved beyond the need for a moral consensus. This assessment is not only narcissistic, but it is just plain wrong. The symptoms of a society that suffers from a deficiency of scruples are prominently and painfully displayed to the dismay of self-appointed experts. Divorce, abortion, crime, pornography, substance abuse, and corruption at the highest levels of national and international government are lamentable signs of the times. However, it is here that we can become that substance that preserves life in a dying world. It is at the present moment that we can shine as beacons, to light the way for a lost people.

Lastly, we cannot stand idly by and watch the plans of internationalists collide with individual freedoms. Thousands of years ago, the ancient Hebrew prophet Isaiah warned Israel of a future time where some would call evil good and good evil.[8] We witness this type of moral confusion occurring in all strata of our culture, but as we have seen, this is particularly true at the international level. We cannot be silent and allow the coercive population control agenda to sweep the world. We cannot allow the inalienable right to life to be replaced with the sanctioning of its termination. The intimate decisions involving our families and our private pursuits must be protected from international influence. The definitions of marriage, family, and parenting, must be preserved in their original, divinely-inspired statuses. Environmentalism must not be used as a pretext to destroy our freedoms, and perhaps our very civilization. We must cherish nature as part of the Creator's design, but refuse to allow the earth to become an idol of worship. We were given dominion over the earth, but care, compassion, and responsibility must be shown in relation to all of creation. We must defend liberty and preserve our nation for the sake of our forefathers and the future of our children's children. This grand design must not be allowed to slip away.

Most of all, in everything, we must pray, as our founding fathers did. When our people rely upon His providence once again, He will preserve and revive our nation. We must return to the humble and prayerful spirit and follow the Old Testament precepts: "If my people, who are called by My name, will humble themselves and pray and seek My face and turn from their wicked ways, then will I hear from heaven and will forgive their sin and will heal their land."[9]

Notes

1. Revelation 13.

2. John 18: 36.

3. Jan Pit, *Persecution: It Will Never Happen Here?* (Orange, CA: Open Doors, 1981), 17.

4. Matthew 10: 16.

5. Matthew 5: 13.

6. C.S. Lewis, *God in the Dock* (Grand Rapids, MI: Eerdmans, 1971), 262.

7. Romans 13:1; Titus 3:1.

8. Isaiah 5:20.

9. 2 Chronicles 7:14 (NIV).

The
Declaration of Independence

The Unanimous Declaration of the Thirteen United States of America

When in the course of human events, it becomes necessary for one people to dissolve the political bands which have connected them with another, and to assume among the powers of the earth, the separate and equal station to which the laws of nature and of nature's God entitles them, a decent respect to the opinions of mankind requires that they should declare the causes which impel them to the separation.

We hold these truths to be self-evident, that all men are created equal, that they are endowed by their Creator with certain unalienable rights, that among these are life, liberty and the pursuit of happiness. That to secure these rights, governments are instituted among men, deriving their just powers from the consent of the governed. That whenever any form of government becomes destructive of these ends, it is the right of the people to alter or to abolish it, and to institute new government, laying its foundation on such principles and organizing its powers in such form, as to them shall seem most likely to effect their safety and happiness. Prudence, indeed, will dictate that governments long established should not be changed for light and transient causes; and accordingly all experience hath shown that mankind are more disposed to suffer, while evils are sufferable, than to right themselves by abolishing the forms to which they are accustomed. But when a long train of abuses and usurpations, pursuing invariably the same object evinces a design to reduce them under absolute despotism, it is their right, it is their duty, to throw off such government, and to provide new guards for their future security. Such has been the patient sufferance of these colonies; and such is now the necessity which constrains them to alter their former systems of governments. The history of the present King of Great Britain is a history of repeated injuries and usurpations, all having in direct object the establishment of an absolute tyranny over these states. To prove this, let facts be submitted to a candid world.

He has refused his assent to laws, the most wholesome and necessary for the public good.

He has forbidden his governors to pass laws of immediate and pressing importance, unless suspended in their operation till his assent should be obtained; and when so suspended, he has utterly neglected to attend to them.

He has refused to pass other laws for the accommodation of large districts of people, unless those people would relinquish the right of representation in the legislature, a right inestimable to them and formidable to tyrants only.

He has called together legislative bodies at places unusual, uncomfortable, and distant from the depository of their public records, for the sole purpose of fatiguing them into compliance with his measures.

He has dissolved representative houses repeatedly, for opposing with manly firmness his invasion on the rights of the people.

He has refused for a long time, after such dissolutions, to cause others to be elected; whereby the legislative powers, incapable of annihilation, have returned to the people at large for their exercise; the state remaining in the meantime exposed to all the dangers of invasion from without, and convulsions within.

He has endeavored to prevent the population of these states; for that purpose obstructing the laws for naturalization of foreigners; refusing to pass others to encourage their migrations hither, and raising the conditions of new appropriations of lands.

He has obstructed the administration of justice, by refusing his assent to laws for establishing judiciary powers.

He has made judges dependent on his will alone, for the tenure of their offices, and the amount and payment of their salaries.

He has erected a multitude of new offices, and sent hither swarms of officers to harass our people, and eat out their substance.

He has kept among us, in times of peace, standing armies without the consent of our legislature.

He has affected to render the military independent of and superior to the civil power.

He has combined with others to subject us to a jurisdiction foreign to our constitution, and unacknowledged by our laws; giving his assent to their acts of pretended legislation:

For quartering large bodies of armed troops among us:

For protecting them, by a mock trial, from punishment for any murders which they should commit on the inhabitants of these states:

For cutting off our trade with all parts of the world:

For imposing taxes on us without our consent:

For depriving us in many cases, of the benefits of trial by jury:

For transporting us beyond seas to be tried for pretended offenses:

For abolishing the free system of English laws in a neighboring province, establishing therein an arbitrary government, and enlarging its boundaries so as to render it at once an example and fit instrument for introducing the same absolute rule into these colonies:

For taking away our charters, abolishing our most valuable laws, and altering fundamentally the forms of our government:

For suspending our own legislatures, and declaring themselves invested with power to legislate for us in all cases whatsoever.

He has abdicated government here, by declaring us out of his protection and waging war against us.

He has plundered our seas, ravaged our coasts, burnt our towns, and destroyed the lives of our people.

He is at this time transporting large armies of foreign mercenaries to complete the works of death, desolation and tyranny, already begun with circumstances of cruelty and perfidy scarcely paralleled in the most barbarous ages, and totally unworthy the head of a civilized nation.

He has constrained our fellow citizens taken captive on the high seas to bear arms against their country, to become the executioners of their friends and brethren, or to fall themselves by their hands.

He has excited domestic insurrections amongst us, and has endeavored to bring on the inhabitants of our frontiers, the merciless Indian savages, whose known rule of warfare, is an undistinguished destruction of all ages, sexes and conditions.

In every stage of these suppressions we have petitioned for redress in the most humble terms: our repeated petitions have been answered only by repeated injury. A prince, whose character is thus marked by every act which may define a tyrant, is unfit to be the ruler of a free people.

Nor have we been wanting in attention to our British brethren. We have warned them from time to time of attempts by their legislature to extend an unwarrantable jurisdiction over us. We have reminded them of the circumstances of our emigration and settlement here. We have appealed to their native justice and magnanimity, and we have conjured them by the ties of our common kindred to disavow these usurpations, which would inevitably interrupt our connections and correspondence. They too have been deaf to the voice of justice and of consanguinity. We must, therefore, acquiesce in the necessity, which denounces our separation, and hold them, as we hold the rest of mankind, enemies in war, in peace friends.

We, therefore, the representatives of the United States of America, in General Congress, assembled, appealing to the Supreme Judge of the world for the rectitude of our intentions, do, in the name, and by the authority of the good people of these colonies, solemnly publish and declare, that these united colonies are, and of right ought to be free and independent states; that they are absolved from all allegiance to the British Crown, and that all political connection between them and the state of Great Britain, is and ought to be totally dissolved; and that as free and independent states, they have full power to levy war, conclude peace, contract alliance, establish commerce, and to do all other acts and things which independent states may of right do. And for the support of this declaration, with a firm reliance on the protection of Divine Providence, we mutually pledge to each other our lives, our fortunes and our sacred honor.

The Constitution of the United States of America

Preamble to the Constitution of the United States

We the people of the United States, in order to form a more perfect union, establish justice, insure domestic tranquility, provide for the common defense, promote the general welfare, and secure the blessings of liberty to ourselves and our posterity, do ordain and establish this Constitution for the United States of America.

Article I

Section 1.

All legislative powers herein granted shall be vested in a Congress of the United States, which shall consist of a Senate and House of Representatives.

Section 2.

The House of Representatives shall be composed of members chosen every second year by the people of the several states, and the electors in each state shall have the qualifications requisite for electors of the most numerous branch of the state legislature.

No person shall be a Representative who shall not have attained to the age of twenty-five years, and been seven years a citizen of the United States, and who shall not, when elected, be an inhabitant of that state in which he shall be chosen.

Representatives and direct taxes shall be apportioned among the several states which may be included within this union, according to their respective numbers, which shall be determined by adding to the whole number of free persons, including those bound to service for a term of years, and excluding Indians not taxed, three fifths of all other Persons. The actual Enumeration shall be made within three years after the first meeting of the Congress of the United States, and within every subsequent term of ten years, in such manner as they shall by law direct. The number of Representatives shall not exceed one for every thirty thousand, but each state shall have at least one Representative; and until such enumeration shall be made, the state of New Hampshire shall be entitled to choose three, Massachusetts eight, Rhode Island and Providence Plantations one, Connecticut five, New York six, New Jersey four,

Pennsylvania eight, Delaware one, Maryland six, Virginia ten, North Carolina five, South Carolina five, and Georgia three.

When vacancies happen in the Representation from any state, the executive authority thereof shall issue writs of election to fill such vacancies.

The House of Representatives shall choose their speaker and other officers; and shall have the sole power of impeachment.

Section 3.

The Senate of the United States shall be composed of two Senators from each state, chosen by the legislature thereof, for six years; and each Senator shall have one vote.

Immediately after they shall be assembled in consequence of the first election, they shall be divided as equally as may be into three classes. The seats of the Senators of the first class shall be vacated at the expiration of the second year, of the second class at the expiration of the fourth year, and of the third class at the expiration of the sixth year, so that one third may be chosen every second year; and if vacancies happen by resignation, or otherwise, during the recess of the legislature of any state, the executive thereof may make temporary appointments until the next meeting of the legislature, which shall then fill such vacancies.

No person shall be a Senator who shall not have attained to the age of thirty years, and been nine years a citizen of the United States and who shall not, when elected, be an inhabitant of that state for which he shall be chosen.

The Vice President of the United States shall be President of the Senate, but shall have no vote, unless they be equally divided.

The Senate shall choose their other officers, and also a President pro tempore, in the absence of the Vice President, or when he shall exercise the office of President of the United States.

The Senate shall have the sole power to try all impeachments. When sitting for that purpose, they shall be on oath or affirmation. When the President of the United States is tried, the Chief Justice shall preside: And no person shall be convicted without the concurrence of two thirds of the members present.

Judgment in cases of impeachment shall not extend further than to removal from office, and disqualification to hold and enjoy any office of honor, trust or profit under the United States: but the party convicted shall nevertheless be liable and subject to indictment, trial, judgment and punishment, according to law.

Section 4.

The times, places and manner of holding elections for Senators and Representatives, shall be prescribed in each state by the legislature thereof; but the Congress may at any time by law make or alter such regulations, except as to the places of choosing Senators.

The Congress shall assemble at least once in every year, and such meeting shall be on the first Monday in December, unless they shall by law appoint a different day.

Section 5.

Each House shall be the judge of the elections, returns and qualifications of its own members, and a majority of each shall constitute a quorum to do business; but a smaller number may adjourn from day to day, and may be authorized to compel the attendance of absent members, in such manner, and under such penalties as each House may provide.

Each House may determine the rules of its proceedings, punish its members for disorderly behavior, and, with the concurrence of two thirds, expel a member.

Each House shall keep a journal of its proceedings, and from time to time publish the same, excepting such parts as may in their judgment require secrecy; and the yeas and nays of the members of either House on any question shall, at the desire of one fifth of those present, be entered on the journal.

Neither House, during the session of Congress, shall, without the consent of the other, adjourn for more than three days, nor to any other place than that in which the two Houses shall be sitting.

Section 6.

The Senators and Representatives shall receive a compensation for their services, to be ascertained by law, and paid out of the treasury of the United States. They shall in all cases, except treason, felony and breach of the peace, be privileged from arrest during their attendance at the session of their respective Houses, and in going to and returning from the same; and for any speech or debate in either House, they shall not be questioned in any other place.

No Senator or Representative shall, during the time for which he was elected, be appointed to any civil office under the authority of the United States, which shall have been created, or the emoluments whereof shall have been increased during such time: and no person holding any office under the United States, shall be a member of either House during his continuance in office.

Section 7.

All bills for raising revenue shall originate in the House of Representatives; but the Senate may propose or concur with amendments as on other Bills.

Every bill which shall have passed the House of Representatives and the Senate, shall, before it becomes a law, be presented to the President of the United States; if he approve he shall sign it, but if not he shall return it, with his objections to that House in which it shall have originated, who shall enter the objections at large on their journal, and proceed to reconsider it. If after such reconsideration two thirds of that House shall agree to pass the bill, it shall be sent, together with the objections, to the other House, by which it shall likewise be reconsidered, and if approved by two thirds of that House, it shall become a law. But in all such cases the votes of both Houses shall be determined by yeas and nays, and the names of the persons voting for and against the bill shall be entered on the journal of each House respectively. If any bill shall not be returned by the President within ten days (Sundays excepted) after it shall have been presented to him, the same shall be a law, in like manner as if he had signed it, unless the Congress by their adjournment prevent its return, in which case it shall not be a law.

Every order, resolution, or vote to which the concurrence of the Senate and House of Representatives may be necessary (except on a question of adjournment) shall be presented to the President of the United States; and before the same shall take effect, shall be approved by him, or being disapproved by him, shall be repassed by two thirds of the Senate and House of Representatives, according to the rules and limitations prescribed in the case of a bill.

Section 8.

The Congress shall have power to lay and collect taxes, duties, imposts and excises, to pay the debts and provide for the common defense and general welfare of the United States; but all duties, imposts and excises shall be uniform throughout the United States;

To borrow money on the credit of the United States;

To regulate commerce with foreign nations, and among the several states, and with the Indian tribes;

To establish a uniform rule of naturalization, and uniform laws on the subject of bankruptcies throughout the United States;

To coin money, regulate the value thereof, and of foreign coin, and fix the standard of weights and measures;

To provide for the punishment of counterfeiting the securities and current coin of the United States;

To establish post offices and post roads;

To promote the progress of science and useful arts, by securing for limited times to authors and inventors the exclusive right to their respective writings and discoveries;

To constitute tribunals inferior to the Supreme Court;

To define and punish piracies and felonies committed on the high seas, and offenses against the law of nations;

To declare war, grant letters of marque and reprisal, and make rules concerning captures on land and water;

To raise and support armies, but no appropriation of money to that use shall be for a longer term than two years;

To provide and maintain a navy;

To make rules for the government and regulation of the land and naval forces;

To provide for calling forth the militia to execute the laws of the union, suppress insurrections and repel invasions;

To provide for organizing, arming, and disciplining, the militia, and for governing such part of them as may be employed in the service of the United States, reserving to the states respectively, the appointment of the officers, and the authority of training the militia according to the discipline prescribed by Congress;

To exercise exclusive legislation in all cases whatsoever, over such District (not exceeding ten miles square) as may, by cession of particular states, and the acceptance of Congress, become the seat of the government of the United States, and to exercise like authority over all places purchased by the consent of the legislature of the state in which the same shall be, for the erection of forts, magazines, arsenals, dockyards, and other needful buildings; And

To make all laws which shall be necessary and proper for carrying into execution the foregoing powers, and all other powers vested by this Constitution in the government of the United States, or in any department or officer thereof.

Section 9.

The migration or importation of such persons as any of the states now existing shall think proper to admit, shall not be prohibited by the Congress prior to the year one thousand eight hundred and eight, but a tax or duty may be imposed on such importation, not exceeding ten dollars for each person.

The privilege of the writ of *habeas corpus* shall not be suspended, unless when in cases of rebellion or invasion the public safety may require it.

No bill of attainder or *ex post facto* Law shall be passed.

No capitation, or other direct, tax shall be laid, unless in proportion to the census or enumeration herein before directed to be taken.

No tax or duty shall be laid on articles exported from any state.

No preference shall be given by any regulation of commerce or revenue to the ports of one state over those of another: nor shall vessels bound to, or from, one state, be obliged to enter, clear or pay duties in another.

No money shall be drawn from the treasury, but in consequence of appropriations made by law; and a regular statement and account of the receipts and expenditures of all public money shall be published from time to time.

No title of nobility shall be granted by the United States: and no person holding any office of profit or trust under them, shall, without

the consent of the Congress, accept of any present, emolument, office, or title, of any kind whatever, from any king, prince, or foreign state.
Section 10.

No state shall enter into any treaty, alliance, or confederation; grant letters of marque and reprisal; coin money; emit bills of credit; make anything but gold and silver coin a tender in payment of debts; pass any bill of attainder, *ex post facto* law, or law impairing the obligation of contracts, or grant any title of nobility.

No state shall, without the consent of the Congress, lay any imposts of duties on imports or exports, except what may be absolutely necessary for executing its inspection laws: and the net produce of all duties and imposts, laid by any state on imports or exports, shall be for the use of the treasury of the United States; and all such laws shall be subject to the revision and control of the Congress.

No state shall, without the consent of Congress, lay any duty of tonnage, keep troops, or ships of war in time of peace, enter into any agreement or compact with another state, or with a foreign power, or engage in war, unless actually invaded, or in such imminent danger as will not admit of delay.
Article II
Section 1.

The executive power shall be vested in a President of the United States of America. He shall hold his office during the term of four years, and, together with the Vice President, chosen for the same term, be elected, as follows:

Each state shall appoint, in such manner as the Legislature thereof may direct, a number of electors, equal to the whole number of Senators and Representatives to which the State may be entitled in the Congress: but no Senator or Representative, or person holding an office of trust or profit under the United States, shall be appointed an elector.

The electors shall meet in their respective states, and vote by ballot for two persons, of whom one at least shall not be an inhabitant of the same state with themselves. And they shall make a list of all the persons voted for, and of the number of votes for each; which list they shall sign and certify, and transmit sealed to the seat of the government of the United States, directed to the President of the Senate. The President of the Senate shall, in the presence of the Senate and House of Representatives, open all the certificates, and the votes shall then be counted. The person having the greatest number of votes shall be the President, if such number be a majority of the whole number of electors appointed; and if there be more than one who have such majority, and have an equal number of votes, then the House of Representatives shall immediately choose by ballot one of them for President; and if no person have a majority, then from the five highest on the list the said House shall in like manner choose the President. But in choosing the President, the votes shall be taken by States, the representation from each state having one vote; A quorum for this purpose shall consist of a member or members from two thirds of the states, and a majority of all the states shall be necessary to a choice. In every case, after the choice of the President, the person having the greatest number of votes of the electors shall be the Vice President. But if there should remain two or more who have equal votes, the Senate shall choose from them by ballot the Vice President.

The Congress may determine the time of choosing the electors, and the day on which they shall give their votes; which day shall be the same throughout the United States.

No person except a natural born citizen, or a citizen of the United States, at the time of the adoption of this Constitution, shall be eligible to the office of President; neither shall any person be eligible to that office who shall not have attained to the age of thirty five years, and been fourteen years a resident within the United States.

In case of the removal of the President from office, or of his death, resignation, or inability to discharge the powers and duties of the said office, the same shall devolve on the Vice President, and the Congress may by law provide for the case of removal, death, resignation or inability, both of the President and Vice President, declaring what officer shall then act as President, and such officer shall act accordingly, until the disability be removed, or a President shall be elected.

The President shall, at stated times, receive for his services, a compensation, which shall neither be increased nor diminished during the period for which he shall have been elected, and he shall not receive within that period any other emolument from the United States, or any of them.

Before he enter on the execution of his office, he shall take the following oath or affirmation: "I do solemnly swear (or affirm) that I will faithfully execute the office of President of the United States, and will to the best of my ability, preserve, protect and defend the Constitution of the United States."

Section 2.

The President shall be commander in chief of the Army and Navy of the United States, and of the militia of the several states, when called into the actual service of the United States; he may require the opinion, in writing, of the principal officer in each of the executive departments, upon any subject relating to the duties of their respective offices, and he shall have power to grant reprieves and pardons for offenses against the United States, except in cases of impeachment.

He shall have power, by and with the advice and consent of the Senate, to make treaties, provided two thirds of the Senators present concur; and he shall nominate, and by and with the advice and consent of the Senate, shall appoint ambassadors, other public ministers and consuls, judges of the Supreme Court, and all other officers of the United States, whose appointments are not herein otherwise provided for, and which shall be established by law: but the Congress may by law vest the appointment of such inferior officers, as they think proper, in the President alone, in the courts of law, or in the heads of departments.

The President shall have power to fill up all vacancies that may happen during the recess of the Senate, by granting commissions which shall expire at the end of their next session.

Section 3.

He shall from time to time give to the Congress information of the state of the union, and recommend to their consideration such measures as he shall judge necessary and expedient; he may, on extraordinary occasions, convene both Houses, or either of them, and in case of disagreement between them, with respect to the time of adjournment, he may adjourn them to such time as he shall think proper; he shall receive ambassadors and other public ministers; he shall take care that the laws be faithfully executed, and shall commission all the officers of the United States.

Section 4.

The President, Vice President and all civil officers of the United States, shall be removed from office on impeachment for, and conviction of, treason, bribery, or other high crimes and misdemeanors.

Article III

Section 1.

The judicial power of the United States, shall be vested in one Supreme Court, and in such inferior courts as the Congress may from time to time ordain and establish. The judges, both of the supreme and inferior courts, shall hold their offices during good behaviour, and shall, at stated times, receive for their services, a compensation, which shall not be diminished during their continuance in office.

Section 2.

The judicial power shall extend to all cases, in law and equity, arising under this Constitution, the laws of the United States, and treaties made, or which shall be made, under their authority; to all cases affecting ambassadors, other public ministers and consuls; to all cases of admiralty and maritime jurisdiction; to controversies to which the United States shall be a party; to controversies between two or more states; between a state and citizens of another state; between citizens of different states; between citizens of the same state claiming lands under grants of different states, and between a state, or the citizens thereof, and foreign states, citizens or subjects.

In all cases affecting ambassadors, other public ministers and consuls, and those in which a state shall be party, the Supreme Court shall have original jurisdiction. In all the other cases before mentioned, the Supreme Court shall have appellate jurisdiction, both as to law and fact, with such exceptions, and under such regulations as the Congress shall make.

The trial of all crimes, except in cases of impeachment, shall be by jury; and such trial shall be held in the state where the said crimes shall have been committed; but when not committed within any state, the trial shall be at such place or places as the Congress may by law have directed.

Section 3.

Treason against the United States, shall consist only in levying war against them, or in adhering to their enemies, giving them aid and comfort. No person shall be convicted of treason unless on the testimony of two witnesses to the same overt act, or on confession in open court.

The Congress shall have power to declare the punishment of treason, but no attainder of treason shall work corruption of blood, or forfeiture except during the life of the person attainted.

Article IV

Section 1.

Full faith and credit shall be given in each state to the public acts, records, and judicial proceedings of every other state. And the Congress may by general laws prescribe the manner in which such acts, records, and proceedings shall be proved, and the effect thereof.

Section 2.

The citizens of each state shall be entitled to all privileges and immunities of citizens in the several states.

A person charged in any state with treason, felony, or other crime, who shall flee from justice, and be found in another state, shall on demand of the executive authority of the state from which he fled, be delivered up, to be removed to the state having jurisdiction of the crime.

No person held to service or labor in one state, under the laws thereof, escaping into another, shall, in consequence of any law or regulation therein, be discharged from such service or labor, but shall be delivered up on claim of the party to whom such service or labor may be due.

Section 3.

New states may be admitted by the Congress into this union; but no new states shall be formed or erected within the jurisdiction of any other state; nor any state be formed by the junction of two or more states, or parts of states, without the consent of the legislatures of the states concerned as well as of the Congress.

The Congress shall have power to dispose of and make all needful rules and regulations respecting the territory or other property belonging to the United States; and nothing in this Constitution shall be so construed as to prejudice any claims of the United States, or of any particular state.

Section 4.

The United States shall guarantee to every state in this union a republican form of government, and shall protect each of them against invasion; and on application of the legislature, or of the executive (when the legislature cannot be convened) against domestic violence.

Article V

The Congress, whenever two thirds of both houses shall deem it necessary, shall propose amendments to this Constitution, or, on the application of the legislatures of two thirds of the several states, shall call a convention for proposing amendments, which, in either case, shall be valid to all intents and purposes, as part of this Constitution, when ratified by the legislatures of three fourths of the several states, or by conventions in three fourths thereof, as the one or the other mode of ratification may be proposed by the Congress; provided that no amendment which may be made prior to the year one thousand eight hundred and eight shall in any manner affect the first and fourth clauses in the ninth section of the first article; and that no state, without its consent, shall be deprived of its equal suffrage in the Senate.

Article VI

All debts contracted and engagements entered into, before the adoption of this Constitution, shall be as valid against the United States under this Constitution, as under the Confederation.

This Constitution, and the laws of the United States which shall be made in pursuance thereof; and all treaties made, or which shall be made, under the authority of the United States, shall be the supreme law of the land; and the judges in every state shall be bound thereby, anything in the Constitution or laws of any State to the contrary notwithstanding.

The Senators and Representatives before mentioned, and the members of the several state legislatures, and all executive and judicial officers, both of the United States and of the several states, shall be bound by oath or affirmation, to support this Constitution; but no religious test shall ever be required as a qualification to any office or public trust under the United States.

Article VII

The ratification of the conventions of nine states, shall be sufficient for the establishment of this Constitution between the states so ratifying the same.

Done in convention by the unanimous consent of the states present the seventeenth day of September in the year of our Lord one thousand seven hundred and eighty seven and of the independence of the United States of America the twelfth.

Amendments to the Constitution of the United States

Amendment I (1791)

Congress shall make no law respecting an establishment of religion, or prohibiting the free exercise thereof; or abridging the freedom of speech, or of the press; or the right of the people peaceably to assemble, and to petition the government for a redress of grievances.

Amendment II (1791)

A well regulated militia, being necessary to the security of a free state, the right of the people to keep and bear arms, shall not be infringed.

Amendment III (1791)

No soldier shall, in time of peace be quartered in any house, without the consent of the owner, nor in time of war, but in a manner to be prescribed by law.

Amendment IV (1791)

The right of the people to be secure in their persons, houses, papers, and effects, against unreasonable searches and seizures, shall not be violated, and no warrants shall issue, but upon probable cause, supported by oath or affirmation, and particularly describing the place to be searched, and the persons or things to be seized.

Amendment V (1791)

No person shall be held to answer for a capital, or otherwise infamous crime, unless on a presentment or indictment of a grand jury, except in cases arising in the land or naval forces, or in the militia, when in actual service in time of war or public danger; nor shall any person be subject for the same offense to be twice put in jeopardy of life or limb; nor shall be compelled in any criminal case to be a witness against himself, nor be deprived of life, liberty, or property, without due process of law; nor shall private property be taken for public use, without just compensation.

Amendment VI (1791)

In all criminal prosecutions, the accused shall enjoy the right to a speedy and public trial, by an impartial jury of the state and district wherein the crime shall have been committed, which district shall have been previously ascertained by law, and to be informed of the nature and cause of the accusation; to be confronted with the witnesses against him; to have compulsory process for obtaining witnesses in his favor, and to have the assistance of counsel for his defense.

Amendment VII (1791)

In suits at common law, where the value in controversy shall exceed twenty dollars, the right of trial by jury shall be preserved, and no fact tried by a jury, shall be otherwise reexamined in any court of the United States, than according to the rules of the common law.

Amendment VIII (1791)

Excessive bail shall not be required, nor excessive fines imposed, nor cruel and unusual punishments inflicted.

Amendment IX (1791)

The enumeration in the Constitution, of certain rights, shall not be construed to deny or disparage others retained by the people.

Amendment X (1791)

The powers not delegated to the United States by the Constitution, nor prohibited by it to the states, are reserved to the states respectively, or to the people.

Amendment XI (1798)

The judicial power of the United States shall not be construed to extend to any suit in law or equity, commenced or prosecuted against one of the United States by citizens of another state, or by citizens or subjects of any foreign state.

Amendment XII (1804)

The electors shall meet in their respective states and vote by ballot for President and Vice-President, one of whom, at least, shall not be an inhabitant of the same state with themselves; they shall name in their ballots the person voted for as President, and in distinct ballots the person voted for as Vice-President, and they shall make distinct lists of all persons voted for as President, and of all persons voted for as Vice-President, and of the number of votes for each, which lists they shall sign and certify, and transmit sealed to the seat of the government of the United States, directed to the President of the Senate; The President of the Senate shall, in the presence of the Senate and House of Representatives, open all the certificates and the votes shall then be counted; the person having the greatest number of votes for President, shall be the President, if such number be a majority of the whole number of electors appointed; and if no person have such majority, then from the persons having the highest numbers not exceeding three on the list of those voted for as President, the House of Representatives shall choose immediately, by ballot, the President. But in choosing the President, the votes shall be taken by states, the representation from each state having one vote; a quorum for this purpose shall consist of a member or members from two-thirds of the states, and a majority of all the states shall be necessary to a choice. And if the House of Representatives shall not choose a President whenever the right of choice shall devolve upon them, before the fourth day of March next following, then the Vice-

President shall act as President, as in the case of the death or other constitutional disability of the President. The person having the greatest number of votes as Vice-President, shall be the Vice-President, if such number be a majority of the whole number of electors appointed, and if no person have a majority, then from the two highest numbers on the list, the Senate shall choose the Vice-President; a quorum for the purpose shall consist of two-thirds of the whole number of Senators, and a majority of the whole number shall be necessary to a choice. But no person constitutionally ineligible to the office of President shall be eligible to that of Vice-President of the United States.

Amendment XIII (1865)

Section 1.

Neither slavery nor involuntary servitude, except as a punishment for crime whereof the party shall have been duly convicted, shall exist within the United States, or any place subject to their jurisdiction.

Section 2.

Congress shall have power to enforce this article by appropriate legislation.

Amendment XIV (1868)

Section 1.

All persons born or naturalized in the United States, and subject to the jurisdiction thereof, are citizens of the United States and of the state wherein they reside. No state shall make or enforce any law which shall abridge the privileges or immunities of citizens of the United States; nor shall any state deprive any person of life, liberty, or property, without due process of law; nor deny to any person within its jurisdiction the equal protection of the laws.

Section 2.

Representatives shall be apportioned among the several states according to their respective numbers, counting the whole number of persons in each state, excluding Indians not taxed. But when the right to vote at any election for the choice of electors for President and Vice President of the United States, Representatives in Congress, the executive and judicial officers of a state, or the members of the legislature thereof, is denied to any of the male inhabitants of each state, being twenty-one years of age, and citizens of the United States, or in any way abridged, except for participation in rebellion, or other crime, the basis of representation therein shall be reduced in the proportion which the number of such male citizens shall bear to the whole number of male citizens twenty-one years of age in such state.

Section 3.

No person shall be a Senator or Representative in Congress, or elector of President and Vice President, or hold any office, civil or military, under the United States, or under any state, who, having previously taken an oath, as a member of Congress, or as an officer of the United States, or as a member of any state legislature, or as an executive or judicial officer of any state, to support the Constitution of the United States, shall have engaged in insurrection or rebellion against the same, or given aid or comfort to the enemies thereof. But Congress may by a vote of two-thirds of each House, remove such disability.

Section 4.

The validity of the public debt of the United States, authorized by law, including debts incurred for payment of pensions and bounties for services in suppressing insurrection or rebellion, shall not be questioned. But neither the United States nor any state shall assume or pay any debt or obligation incurred in aid of insurrection or rebellion against the United States, or any claim for the loss or emancipation of any slave; but all such debts, obligations and claims shall be held illegal and void.

Section 5.

The Congress shall have power to enforce, by appropriate legislation, the provisions of this article.

Amendment XV (1870)

Section 1.

The right of citizens of the United States to vote shall not be denied or abridged by the United States or by any state on account of race, color, or previous condition of servitude.

Section 2.

The Congress shall have power to enforce this article by appropriate legislation.

Amendment XVI (1913)

The Congress shall have power to lay and collect taxes on incomes, from whatever source derived, without apportionment among the several states, and without regard to any census of enumeration.

Amendment XVII (1913)

The Senate of the United States shall be composed of two Senators from each state, elected by the people thereof, for six years; and each Senator shall have one vote. The electors in each state shall have the qualifications requisite for electors of the most numerous branch of the state legislatures.

When vacancies happen in the representation of any state in the Senate, the executive authority of such state shall issue writs of election to fill such vacancies: Provided, that the legislature of any state may empower the executive thereof to make temporary appointments until the people fill the vacancies by election as the legislature may direct.

This amendment shall not be so construed as to affect the election or term of any Senator chosen before it becomes valid as a part of the Constitution.

Amendment XVIII (1919)

Section 1.

After one year from the ratification of this article the manufacture, sale, or transportation of intoxicating liquors within, the importation thereof into, or the exportation thereof from the United States and all territory subject to the jurisdiction thereof for beverage purposes is hereby prohibited.

Section 2.

The Congress and the several states shall have concurrent power to enforce this article by appropriate legislation.

Section 3.

This article shall be inoperative unless it shall have been ratified as an amendment to the Constitution by the legislatures of the several states, as provided in the Constitution, within seven years from the date of the submission hereof to the states by the Congress.

Amendment XIX (1920)

The right of citizens of the United States to vote shall not be denied or abridged by the United States or by any state on account of sex.

Congress shall have power to enforce this article by appropriate legislation.

Amendment XX (1933)

Section 1.

The terms of the President and Vice President shall end at noon on the 20th day of January, and the terms of Senators and Representatives at noon on the 3d day of January, of the years in which such terms would have ended if this article had not been ratified; and the terms of their successors shall then begin.

Section 2.

The Congress shall assemble at least once in every year, and such meeting shall begin at noon on the 3d day of January, unless they shall by law appoint a different day.

Section 3.

If, at the time fixed for the beginning of the term of the President, the President elect shall have died, the Vice President elect shall become President. If a President shall not have been chosen before the time fixed for the beginning of his term, or if the President elect shall have failed to qualify, then the Vice President elect shall act as President until a President shall have qualified; and the Congress may by law provide for the case wherein neither a President elect nor a Vice President elect shall have qualified, declaring who shall then act as President, or the manner in which one who is to act shall be selected, and such person shall act accordingly until a President or Vice President shall have qualified.

Section 4.

The Congress may by law provide for the case of the death of any of the persons from whom the House of Representatives may choose a President whenever the right of choice shall have devolved upon them, and for the case of the death of any of the persons from whom the Senate may choose a Vice President whenever the right of choice shall have devolved upon them.

Section 5.

Sections 1 and 2 shall take effect on the 15th day of October following the ratification of this article.

Section 6.

This article shall be inoperative unless it shall have been ratified as an amendment to the Constitution by the legislatures of three-fourths of the several states within seven years from the date of its submission.

Amendment XXI (1933)

Section 1.

The eighteenth article of amendment to the Constitution of the United States is hereby repealed.

Section 2.

The transportation or importation into any state, territory, or possession of the United States for delivery or use therein of intoxicating liquors, in violation of the laws thereof, is hereby prohibited.

Section 3.

This article shall be inoperative unless it shall have been ratified as an amendment to the Constitution by conventions in the several states, as provided in the Constitution, within seven years from the date of the submission hereof to the states by the Congress.

Amendment XXII (1951)

Section 1.

No person shall be elected to the office of the President more than twice, and no person who has held the office of President, or acted as President, for more than two years of a term to which some other person was elected President shall be elected to the office of the President more than once. But this article shall not apply to any person holding the office of President when this article was proposed by the Congress, and shall not prevent any person who may be holding the office of President, or acting as President, during the term within which this article becomes operative from holding the office of President or acting as President during the remainder of such term.

Section 2.

This article shall be inoperative unless it shall have been ratified as an amendment to the Constitution by the legislatures of three-fourths of the several states within seven years from the date of its submission to the states by the Congress.

Amendment XXIII (1961)

Section 1.

The District constituting the seat of government of the United States shall appoint in such manner as the Congress may direct:

A number of electors of President and Vice President equal to the whole number of Senators and Representatives in Congress to which the District would be entitled if it were a state, but in no event more than the least populous state; they shall be in addition to those appointed by the states, but they shall be considered, for the purposes of the election of President and Vice President, to be electors appointed by a state; and they shall meet in the District and perform such duties as provided by the twelfth article of amendment.

Section 2.

The Congress shall have power to enforce this article by appropriate legislation.

Amendment XXIV (1964)

Section 1.

The right of citizens of the United States to vote in any primary or other election for President or Vice President, for electors for President or Vice President, or for Senator or Representative in Congress, shall not be denied or abridged by the United States or any state by reason of failure to pay any poll tax or other tax.

Section 2.

The Congress shall have power to enforce this article by appropriate legislation.

Amendment XXV (1967)

Section 1.

In case of the removal of the President from office or of his death or resignation, the Vice-President shall become President.

Section 2.

Whenever there is a vacancy in the office of the Vice President, the President shall nominate a Vice President who shall take office upon confirmation by a majority vote of both Houses of Congress.

Section 3.

Whenever the President transmits to the President pro tempore of the Senate and the Speaker of the House of Representatives his written declaration that he is unable to discharge the powers and duties of his office, and until he transmits to them a written declaration to the contrary, such powers and duties shall be discharged by the Vice President as Acting President.

Section 4.

Whenever the Vice President and a majority of either the principal officers of the executive departments or of such other body as Congress may by law provide, transmit to the President pro tempore of the Senate and the Speaker of the House of Representatives their written declaration that the President is unable to discharge the powers and duties of his office, the Vice President shall immediately assume the powers and duties of the office as Acting President.

Thereafter, when the President transmits to the President pro tempore of the Senate and the Speaker of the House of Representatives his written declaration that no inability exists, he shall resume the powers and duties of his office unless the Vice President and a majority of either the principal officers of the executive department or of such other body as Congress may by law provide, transmit within four days to the President pro tempore of the Senate and the Speaker of the House of Representatives their written declaration that the President is unable to discharge the powers and duties of his office. Thereupon Congress shall decide the issue, assembling within forty-eight hours for that purpose if not in session. If the Congress, within twenty-one days after receipt of the latter written declaration, or, if Congress is not in session, within twenty-one days after Congress is required to assemble, determines by two-thirds vote of both Houses that the President is unable to discharge the powers and duties of his office, the Vice President shall continue to discharge the same as Acting President; otherwise, the President shall resume the powers and duties of his office.

Amendment XXVI (1971)

Section 1.

The right of citizens of the United States, who are 18 years of age or older, to vote, shall not be denied or abridged by the United States or any state on account of age.

Section 2.

The Congress shall have the power to enforce this article by appropriate legislation.

Amendment XXVII (1992)

No law varying the compensation for the services of the Senators and Representatives shall take effect until an election of Representatives shall have intervened.

Excerpts from International Covenant on Civil and Political Rights

The States Parties to the present Covenant,

Considering that, in accordance with the principles proclaimed in the Charter of the United Nations, recognition of the inherent dignity and of the equal and inalienable rights of all members of the human family is the foundation of freedom, justice and peace in the world,

Recognizing that these rights derive from the inherent dignity of the human person,

Recognizing that, in accordance with the Universal Declaration of Human Rights, the ideal of free human beings enjoying civil and political freedom and freedom from fear and want can only be achieved if conditions are created whereby everyone may enjoy his civil and political rights, as well as his economic, social and cultural rights,

Considering the obligation of States under the Charter of the United Nations to promote universal respect for and observance of, human rights and freedoms,

Realizing that the individual, having duties to other individuals and to the community to which he belongs, is under a responsibility to strive for the promotion and observance of the rights recognized in the present Covenant,

Agree upon the following articles:

Article 4

1. In time of public emergency which threatens the life of the nation and the existence of which is officially proclaimed, the States Parties to the present Covenant may take measures derogating from their obligations under the present Covenant to the extent strictly required by the exigencies of the situation, provided that such measures are not inconsistent with their other obligations under international law and do not involve discrimination solely on the ground of race, colour, sex, language, religion or social origin.

Article 8

1. No one shall be held in slavery; slavery and the slave-trade in all their forms shall be prohibited.

2. No one shall be held in servitude.

3. (a) No one shall be required to perform forced or compulsory labour

(b) Paragraph 3 (a) shall not be held to preclude, in countries where imprisonment with hard labour may be imposed as a punishment for a crime, the performance of hard labour in pursuance of a sentence to such punishment by a competent court.

(c) For the purpose of this paragraph the term "forced or compulsory labour" shall not include:

(i) Any work or service, not referred to in sub-paragraph (b), normally required of a person who is under detention in consequence of a lawful order of a court, or of a person during conditional release from such detention;

(ii) Any service of a military character and, in countries where conscientious objection is recognized, any national service required by law of conscientious objectors;

(iii) Any service exacted in cases of emergency or calamity threatening the life or well-being of the community;

(iv) Any work or service which forms part of normal civil obligations.

Article 9

1. Everyone has the right to liberty and security of person. No one shall be subjected to arbitrary arrest or detention. No one shall be deprived of his liberty except on such grounds and in accordance with such procedure as are established by law.

Article 12

1. Everyone lawfully within the territory of a State shall, within that territory, have the right to liberty of movement and freedom to choose his residence.

2. Everyone shall be free to leave any country, including his own.

3. The above-mentioned rights shall not be subject to any restrictions except those which are provided by law, are necessary to protect national security, public order (*ordre public*), public health or morals or the rights and freedoms of others, and are consistent with the other rights recognized in the present Covenant.

Article 18

1. Everyone shall have the right to freedom of thought, conscience and religion.

This right shall include freedom to have or to adopt a religion or belief of his choice, and freedom, either individually or in community with others and in public or private, to manifest his religion or belief in worship, observance, practice and teaching.

2. No one shall be subject to coercion which would impair his freedom to have or to adopt a religion or belief of his choice.

3. Freedom to manifest one's religion or beliefs may be subject only to such limitations as are prescribed by law and are necessary to protect public safety, order, health, or morals or the fundamental rights and freedoms of others.

4. The States Parties to the present Covenant undertake to have respect for the liberty of parents and, when applicable, legal guardians to ensure the religious and moral education of their children in conformity with their own convictions.

Article 19

1. Everyone shall have the right to hold opinions without interference.

2. Everyone shall have the right to freedom of expression; this right shall include freedom to seek, receive and impart information and ideas of all kinds, regardless of frontiers, either orally, in writing or in print, in the form of art, or through any other media of his choice.

3. The exercise of the rights provided for in paragraph 2 of this article carries with it special duties and responsibilities. It may therefore be subject to certain restrictions, but these shall only be such as are provided by law and are necessary:

(a) For respect of the rights or reputations of others;

(b) For the protection of national security or of public order (ordre public), or of public health or morals.

Article 20

1. Any propaganda for war shall be prohibited by law.

2. Any advocacy of national, racial or religious hatred that constitutes incitement to discrimination, hostility or violence shall be prohibited by law.

Article 21

The right of peaceful assembly shall be recognized. No restrictions may be placed on the exercise of this right other than those imposed in conformity with the law and which are necessary in a democratic society in the interests of national security or public safety, public order (ordre public), the protection of public health or morals or the protection of the rights and freedoms of others.

Article 22

1. Everyone shall have the right to freedom of association with others, including the right to form and join trade unions for the protection of his interests.

2. No restrictions may be placed on the exercise of this right other than those which are prescribed by law and which are necessary in a democratic society in the interests of national security or public safety, public order (*ordre public*), the protection of public health or morals or the protection of the rights and freedoms of others. This article shall not

prevent the imposition of lawful restrictions on members of the armed forces and of the police in their exercise of this right.

Article 24

1. Every child shall have, without any discrimination as to race, colour, sex, language, religion, national or social origin, property or birth, the right to such measures of protection as are required by his status as a minor, on the part of his family, society and the State.

2. Every child shall be registered immediately after birth and shall have a name.

3. Every child has the right to acquire a nationality.

IN FAITH WHEREOF the undersigned, being duly authorized thereto by their respective Governments, have signed the present Covenant, opened for signature at New York, on the nineteenth day of December, one thousand nine hundred and sixty-six.

Excerpts from the
Charter of the United Nations

CHAPTER VII
ACTION WITH RESPECT TO THREATS TO THE PEACE, BREACHES OF THE
PEACE, AND ACTS OF AGGRESSION

Article 39

The Security Council shall determine the existence of any threat to
the peace, breach of the peace, or act of aggression and shall make
recommendations, or decide what measures shall be taken in accordance
with Articles 41 and 42, to maintain or restore international peace and
security.

Article 40

In order to prevent an aggravation of the situation, the Security
Council may, before making the recommendations or deciding upon the
measures provided for in Article 39, call upon the parties concerned to
comply with such provisional measures as it deems necessary or desirable. Such provisional measures shall be without prejudice to the rights,
claims, or position of the parties concerned. The Security Council shall
duly take account of failure to comply with such provisional measures.

Article 41

The Security Council may decide what measures not involving the
use of armed force are to be employed to give effect to its decisions, and
it may call upon the Members of the United Nations to apply such
measures. These may include complete or partial interruption of economic relations and of rail, sea, air, postal, telegraphic, radio, and other
means of communication, and the severance of diplomatic relations.

Article 42

Should the Security Council consider that measures provided for in
Article 41 would be inadequate or have proved to be inadequate, it may
take such action by air, sea, or land forces as may be necessary to maintain or restore international peace and security. Such action may include
demonstrations, blockade, and other operations by air, sea, or land forces
of Members of the United Nations.

Article 43

1. All Members of the United Nations, in order to contribute to the

maintenance of international peace and security, undertake to make available to the Security Council, on its call and in accordance with a special agreement or agreements, armed forces, assistance, and facilities, including rights of passage, necessary for the purpose of maintaining international peace and security.

2. Such agreement or agreements shall govern the numbers and types of forces, their degree of readiness and general location, and the nature of the facilities and assistance to be provided.

3. The agreement or agreements shall be negotiated as soon as possible on the initiative of the Security Council. They shall be concluded between the Security Council and Members or between the Security Council and groups of Members and shall be subject to ratification by the signatory states in accordance with their respective constitutional processes.

Article 44

When the Security Council has decided to use force it shall, before calling upon a Member not represented on it to provide armed forces in fulfillment of the obligations assumed under Article 43, invite that Member, if the Member so desires, to participate in the decisions of the Security Council concerning the employment of contingents of that Member's armed forces.

Article 45

In order to enable the United Nations to take urgent military measures, Members shall hold immediately available national air-force contingents for combined international enforcement action. The strength and degree of readiness of these contingents and plans for their combined action shall be determined within the limits laid down in the special agreement or agreements referred to in Article 43, by the Security Council with the assistance of the Military Staff Committee.

Article 46

Plans for the application of armed force shall be made by the Security Council with the assistance of the Military Staff Committee.

Article 47

1. There shall be established a Military Staff Committee to advise and assist the Security Council on all questions relating to the Security Council's military requirements for the maintenance of international peace and security, the employment and command of forces placed at its disposal, the regulation of armaments, and possible disarmament.

2. The Military Staff Committee shall consist of the Chiefs of Staff of the permanent members of the Security Council or their representatives. Any Member of the United Nations not permanently represented on the Committee shall be invited by the Committee to be associated with it when the efficient discharge of the Committee's responsibilities requires the participation of that Member in its work.

3. The Military Staff Committee shall be responsible under the Security Council for the strategic direction of any armed forces placed at the disposal of the Security Council. Questions relating to the command of such forces shall be worked out subsequently.

4. The Military Staff Committee, with the authorization of the Security Council and after consultation with appropriate regional agencies, may establish regional subcommittees.

Article 48

1. The action required to carry out the decisions of the Security Council for the maintenance of international peace and security shall be taken by all the Members of the United Nations or by some of them, as the Security Council may determine.

2. Such decisions shall be carried out by the Members of the United Nations directly and through their action in the appropriate international agencies of which they are members.

Article 49

The Members of the United Nations shall join in affording mutual assistance in carrying out the measures decided upon by the Security Council.

Article 50

If preventive or enforcement measures against any state are taken by the Security Council, any other state, whether a Member of the United Nations or not, which finds itself confronted with special economic problems arising from the carrying out of those measures shall have the right to consult the Security Council with regard to a solution of those problems.

Article 51

Nothing in the present Charter shall impair the inherent right of individual or collective self-defense if an armed attack occurs against a Member of the United Nations, until the Security Council has taken measures necessary to maintain international peace and security. Measures taken by Members in the exercise of this right of self-defense shall be immediately reported to the Security Council and shall not in any way affect the authority and responsibility of the Security Council under the present Charter to take at any time such action as it deems necessary in order to maintain or restore international peace and security.

CHAPTER VIII
REGIONAL ARRANGEMENTS

Article 52

1. Nothing in the present Charter precludes the existence of regional arrangements or agencies for dealing with such matters relating to the maintenance of international peace and security as are appropriate for regional action provided that such arrangements or agencies and

their activities are consistent with the Purposes and Principles of the United Nations.

2. The Members of the United Nations entering into such arrangements or constituting such agencies shall make every effort to achieve pacific settlement of local disputes through such regional arrangements or by such regional agencies before referring them to the Security Council.

3. The Security Council shall encourage the development of pacific settlement of local disputes through such regional arrangements or by such regional agencies either on the initiative of the states concerned or by reference from the Security Council.

4. This Article in no way impairs the application of Articles 34 and 35.

Article 53

1. The Security Council shall, where appropriate, utilize such regional arrangements or agencies for enforcement action under its authority. But no enforcement action shall be taken under regional arrangements or by regional agencies without the authorization of the Security Council, with the exception of measures against any enemy state, as defined in paragraph 2 of this Article, provided for pursuant to Article 107 or in regional arrangements directed against renewal of aggressive policy on the part of any such state, until such time as the Organization may, on request of the Governments concerned, be charged with the responsibility for preventing further aggression by such a state.

2. The term enemy state as used in paragraph 1 of this Article applies to any state which during the Second World War has been an enemy of any signatory of the present Charter.

Article 54

The Security Council shall at all times be kept fully informed of activities undertaken or in contemplation under regional arrangements or by regional agencies for the maintenance of international peace and security.

Selected Reading List

Bandarage, Asoka. *Women, Population and Global Crisis: A Political-Economic Analysis.* Highland, New Jersey: Zed Books, 1997.

Barton, David. *The Foundations of American Government.* Aledo, Texas: Wallbuilders Press, 1993.

Barton, David. *Original Intent: The Courts, the Constitution, & Religion.* Aledo, Texas: Wallbuilders Press, 1996.

Barton, David. *Education and the Founding Fathers* (videorecording). Vision Video, 1997.

Beigbeder, Yves. *Management Problems in United Nations Organizations: Reform or Decline?* New York: St. Martin's Press, 1987.

Besant, Annie. *Thought Power, Its Control and Culture.* Wheaton, Illinois: Theosophical Publishing House, 1989.

Blavatsky, Helena Petrovna. *The Secret Doctrine: The Synthesis of Science, Religion and Philosophy.* Wheaton, Illinois: Theosophical Publishing House, 1977.

Blavatsky, Helena Petrovna. *Isis Unveiled.* Wheaton, Illinois: Theosophical Publishing House, 1994.

Brzoska, Michael, ed. *Conversion Survey 1996: Global Disarmament, Demilitarization and Demobilization.* New York: Oxford University Press, 1996.

Buchanan, Patrick J. *The Great Betrayal: How American Sovereignty and Social Justice Are Being Sacrificed to the Gods of the Global Economy.* Boston: Little, Brown & Co., 1998.

Carpenter, Ted Galen, ed. *Delusions of Grandeur: The United Nations and Global Intervention.* Washington, DC: Cato Institute, 1997.

Cohen, Cynthia Price. *Children's Rights in America: United Nations Convention on the Rights of the Child Compared with United States Law.* Chicago: American Bar Association, 1990.

Collins, Susan M., and Barry P. Bosworth, eds. *The New GATT: Implications for the United States.* Washington, DC: Brookings Institution, 1995.

Commission on Global Governance. *Our Global Neighborhood: The Report of the Commission on Global Governance.* New York: Oxford University Press, 1995.

Croll, Elizabeth, et al. *China's One-Child Family Policy.* New York: St. Martin's Press, 1985.

Cromartie, Michael, ed. *The Nine Lives of Population Control.* Grand Rapids, Michigan: Eerdmans Publishing Company, 1995.

Cumbey, Constance. *The Hidden Dangers of the Rainbow: The New Age Movement and Our Coming Age of Barbarism.* Lafayette, Louisiana: Huntington House, 1985.

DeLong, James V. *Property Matters: How Property Rights Are under Assault—And Why You Should Care.* New York: Free Press, 1997.

Durch, William J., ed. *The Evolution of UN Peacekeeping: Case Studies and Comparative Analysis.* New York: St. Martin's Press, 1993.

Eidsmoe, John. *Christianity and the Constitution: The Faith of Our Founding Fathers.* Grand Rapids, Michigan: Baker Book House, 1995.

Ely, James W. *The Guardian of Every Other Right: A Constitutional History of Property Rights (Bicentennial Essays on the Bill of Rights).* New York: Oxford University Press, 1997.

Foreman, Dave. *Confessions of an Eco-Warrior* (audio cassette). Niwot, Colorado: The Audio Press, 1993.

Ghosh, Pradip K., ed. *Disarmament and Development: A Global Perspective.* Westport, Connecticut: Greenwood Publishing Group, 1984.

Ginsburg, Faye D., and Rayna Rapp, eds. *Conceiving the New World Order: The Global Politics of Reproduction.* Berkeley: University of California Press, 1995.

Grant, George. *The Family under Siege: What the New Social Engineers Have in Mind for You and Your Children.* Minneapolis: Bethany House, 1994.

Grant, George. *Immaculate Deception: The Shifting Agenda of Planned Parenthood.* Chicago: Northfield, 1996.

Grigg, William Norman. *Freedom on the Altar.* Appleton, Wisconsin: American Opinion Press, 1995.

Guzman, Ingrid J. *Parent Police: The United Nations Wants Your Children (Salt Series).* Lafayette, Louisiana: Huntington House, 1995.

Hanson, Virginia. *H.P. Blavatsky and the Secret Doctrine.* Wheaton, Illinois: Theosophical Publishing House, 1988.

Hartmann, Betsy. *Reproductive Rights and Wrongs: The Global Politics of Population Control.* Boston: South End Press, 1994.

Hawkins, Craig. *Goddess Worship, Witchcraft and Neo-Paganism.* Grand Rapids, Michigan: Zondervan Publishing House, 1998.

Heywood, V. H., ed. *Global Biodiversity Assessment.* New York: Cambridge University Press, 1996.

Jones, Peter. *Spirit Wars: Pagan Revival in Christian America.* Mukilteo, Washington: WinePress, 1997.

Kasun, Jacqueline. *The War against Population: The Economics and Ideology of Population Control.* San Francisco: Ignatius Press, 1988.

Kincaid, Cliff. *Global Bondage: The UN Plan to Rule the World.* Lafayette, Louisiana: Huntington House, 1995.

Kincaid, Cliff. *Global Taxes for World Government.* Lafayette, Louisiana: Huntington House, 1997.

Lewis, Martin W. *Green Delusions: An Environmentalist Critique of Radical Environmentalism.* Durham, North Carolina: Duke University Press, 1994.

Liagin, Elizabeth. *Excessive Force: Power, Politics, and Population Control.* Washington, DC: Information Project For Africa, 1996.

List, Peter C. *Radical Environmentalism: Philosophy and Tactics.* Belmont, California: Wadsworth Publishing Company, 1993.

Luksik, Peg, and Pamela Hobbs Hoffecker. *Outcome Based Education: The State's Assault on Our Children's Values.* Lafayette, Louisiana: Huntington House, 1996.

Mander, Jerry, and Edward Goldsmith, eds. *The Case against the Global Economy.* San Francisco: Sierra Club Books, 1996.

Manes, Christopher. *Green Rage: Radical Environmentalism and the Unmaking of Civilization.* Boston: Little, Brown & Co., 1991.

Michaelsen, Johanna. *The Beautiful Side of Evil.* Honesdale, Pennsylvania: Caroline House Publications, 1984.

Mills, Joy. *100 Years of Theosophy: A History of the Theosophical Society in America.* Wheaton, Illinois: Theosophical Publishing House, 1987.

Milwertz, Cecilia Nathansen. *Accepting Population Control: Urban Chinese Women and the One-Child Family Policy.* Richmond, Surrey: Curzon Press, 1996.

Nader, Ralph, ed. *The Case against Free Trade: GATT, NAFTA and the Globalization of Corporate Power.* San Francisco: Earth Island Press, 1993.

Neurath, Paul. *From Malthus to the Club of Rome and Back: Problems of Limits to Growth, Population Control, and Migration.* Armonk, New York: M. E. Sharpe, 1994.

Peters, Cynthia, ed. *Collateral Damage: The New World Order at Home and Abroad.* Boston: South End Press, 1991.

Pollot, Mark L. *Grand Theft and Petty Larceny: Property Rights in America.* San Francisco: Pacific Research Institute for the Public, 1993.

Purdy, Laura M. *In Their Best Interest?: The Case against Equal Rights for Children.* Ithaca: Cornell University Press, 1992.

Ray, Dixie Lee, and Lou Guzzo. *Environmental Overkill: Whatever Happened to Common Sense?* Washington, DC: Regnery Publishing, 1993.

Righter, Rosemary. *Utopia Lost: The United Nations and World Order.* Washington, DC: Brookings Institution, 1995.

Smith, Samantha. *Goddess Earth: Exposing the Pagan Agenda of the Environmental Movement.* Lafayette, Louisiana: Huntington House, 1994.

Smith, Samantha, and Brenda Scott. *Trojan Horse: How the New Age Movement Infiltrates the Church.* Lafayette, Louisiana: Huntington House, 1993.

Taylor, Anne. *Annie Besant: A Biography.* New York: Oxford University Press, 1992.

Taylor, Bron Raymond, ed. *Ecological Resistance Movements: The Global Emergence of Radical and Popular Environmentalism.* New York: State University of New York Press, 1995.

United Nations Publication. *Abortion Policies: A Global Review.* New York: United Nations Publications, 1992.

United Nations Publication. *Basic Facts about the United Nations.* New York: United Nations Publications, 1996.

Van Den Haag, Ernest, and John P. Conrad. *The UN In or Out?: A Debate between Ernest Van Den Haag and John P. Conrad.* New York: Plenum Press, 1987.

York, Michael. *The Emerging Network: A Sociology of the New Age and Neo-Pagan Movements.* Lanham, Maryland: Rowman & Littlefield, 1995.

Zimmerman, Michael E. *Contesting Earth's Future: Radical Ecology and Postmodernity.* Berkeley: University of California Press, 1994.

More good books
from Bridger House Publishers:

The Spiritual Laws and Lessons of the Universe

$19.95 + Shipping

382 pages   ISBN: 0-9640104-6-1

For eons of time in your human history, mankind has experienced and existed in blindness about his divine spiritual heritage, that is, his oneness with the Creation. Since the time of the "Fall" from "grace," many have continued to struggle with what is "their" purpose, and why it is so difficult to find and know THE TRUTH. Many, in their ignorance and confusion, have asked themselves why the Creator allows the seemingly unending ruthless and merciless inhumanity of man to continue; why HE allows suffering of children, wars, disease and pestilence and corruption. Often ones simply decide there is no Creator, which only keeps ones ever "separate" from KNOWING HIS PRESENCE WITHIN.

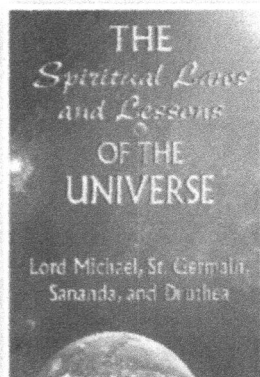

"The Spiritual Laws and Lessons" is deliverance of truth to YOU. The Creator is offering YOU the instructions for reaching the "lighted" path back home to HIM, AND THUS TO ONENESS. You will learn HOW to recognize the Anti-Spirit, (that which is AGAINST the Creator and therefore AGAINST LIFE) within YOU and why through your gift of free-will YOU allowed the Anti-Spirit within your temple. You will learn about what are the "Deadliest" Sins (errors) committed by you and also about the nature of YOUR personal responsibility for ALL consequences and experiences within this manifested physical "illusion."

NOW within these pages bringing forth the EIGHTEEN Logical Cosmic Laws of Balance of The Creation, written in explicit detail with MANY examples given for YOUR careful consideration and recognition of truth. Why? To let there be NO misunderstanding of HOW and WHY you, of humanity, have lost your inner as well as planetary BALANCE. You have broken EVERY law set forth herein and have, therefore, suffered the consequences of your errors against the Creator and against LIFE. You each now have before you YOUR "road map" back home to spiritual wisdom, knowledge and truth. Will YOU see? Will YOU hear? Each ONE of you, being fragments of THE CREATION must and will make this choice: To wisely learn your lessons in truth, abide by the laws and thus EARN your Spiritual UNITY and Freedom within the Kingdom OR continue in the darkness of deception, ignorance and spiritual poverty which will keep you bound in the Anti-Spirit's "illusion" of separation. THIS cycle is about to END. The new cycle will BEGIN anew in the GLORY and Celebration of cleansing within and without of ALL fragments of ANTI-LIFE. WILL YOU JOIN OUR FATHER/MOTHER CREATOR in the Divine Holy Kingdom of LIFE? The Creator awaits your decision. So be it.

To order call 1-800-729-4131

Handbook for the New Paradigm
Volume I

$6.95 + Shipping
192 pages   ISBN: 1-893157-04-0

The messages contained in this handbook are intended to lift mankind from the entrapment of the victim consciousness that keeps the level of experience ensnared in fear and frustration. Humanity was intended to live, not in luxury, but in abundance. The information found in this book will lead all that read and reread with an open mind to the discovery of the truth of who and what they truly are. The end of the search for these answers is provided at last in clarity and conciseness. There are no recriminations or feelings of guilt to be gleaned from these pages. There is clarity and upliftment in each segment. It is the intent and purpose of this small book to encourage every reader to live in accordance with the plainly disclosed simple laws that underlay all that each comprehends as life. Each segment leads to greater understanding and to a simple application that encompasses them in entirety in a few words that guarantee absolute change in your day to day experience.

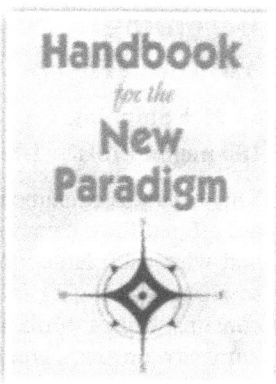

Embracing the Rainbow
Volume II

$6.95 + Shipping
144 pages   ISBN: 1-893157-05-9

Volume II of the Handbook For The New Paradigm contains the continuing series of messages guiding its readers to accept the concepts contained within them for the purpose of creating a new life experience for the "humans becoming" on planet Earth. Each message broadens the conceptual understandings of the necessity to release the limitations that have been thrust upon humanity preventing them from understanding who and what they truly are. It contains surprising truths of some of the shocking deceptions intentionally taught that limit and separate mankind from their opportunities for spiritual evolvement. It defines how it is possible to take back the heritage of self-determination, freely create one's own destiny and heal the planet and humanity as a whole living entity through the suggested dynamic process.

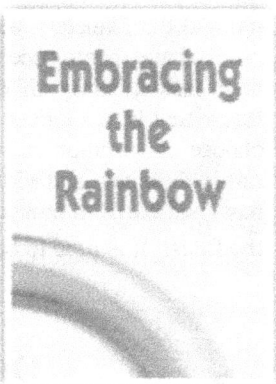

Becoming
Volume III

$6.95 + Shipping
180 pages   ISBN: 1-893157-07-5

The messages contained in this, the third book, are offered for the continued realization of who and what each human being truly is. The consciousness changing information each volume contains brings forth the understanding that humanity on this planet is, in reality, a whole and holy awareness. From the global myriad of belief systems arises a single picture that represents a composite awareness. This totality of thought creates the reality of the human experience, a great deal of effort is now focused with the intent of influencing how the individual and the total global awareness perceive the human experience. The mind discerns what it understands is its surrounding reality but the feelings determine its believability. Confusion masks the ability to choose between what appears to be true and what the feelings believe to be true. Beneath all the rhetoric that is focused on the conscious and subconscious levels within the current deluge of information in all its various forms is the human desire for the freedom to choose what is for the highest and best good of each individual and the planetary whole. Mankind stands at the threshold, the decision point of whether to accept what it is being told is for its highest and best good or to instead shrug off the programmed suggestions and choose for itself a future that is in total contrast. At the heart of the matter is the opportunity to choose cooperation rather than competition, brotherly love and assistance rather than hate and violence. It is time to observe the world situation that has resulted from competition and experiencing the premise of survival of the fittest. It is time to begin.

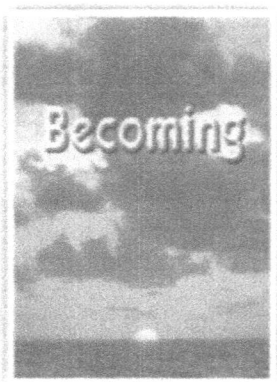

ORDER ENTIRE SET
(Vol. I, II, III)
for $19.95 + Shipping and receive
Messages for the Ground Crew FREE

Call 1-800-729-4131 or www.nohoax.com

For a Free Catalog

of related publications

Call 1-800-729-4131

Visit our website at

www.nohoax.com